The Government is not Your Daddy

THE GOVERNMENT IS NOT YOUR DADDY

A Student's Guide to a
Better America
Part I

STEVEN ROTTER & BRADLEY ROTTER

Library of Congress Control Number:		2010908123
ISBN:	Hardcover	978-1-4535-1486-3
	Softcover	978-1-4535-1485-6
	Ebook	978-1-4535-1487-0

This book was printed in the United States of America.

To order additional copies of this book, contact:
Xlibris Corporation
1-888-795-4274
www.Xlibris.com
Orders@Xlibris.com
81273

CONTENTS

DEDICATION

This book is dedicated to the remarkable founders of our country and all of the men and women who have sacrificed everything in the defense and preservation of our constitution.

It is our sincere hope that we can end the nanny-state mentality and communist-style governance. The America that has been the most innovative, free and generous country in history, is being stolen away at remarkable speed. It is incumbant upon each of us, **individually**, to stop this terrible transformation and restore greatness and real hope for all of us.

INTRODUCTION

And so my fellow Americans, ask not what your country can do for you—ask what you can do for your country.
—Democratic president John F. Kennedy
at his 1961 inaugural address

First and foremost, this book is for kids. More specifically, for students in high school and college. The reason we've chosen to focus on this age group is that this book is about personal responsibility. It is about a return to the idea that your own situation is the result of your own actions and that you shouldn't expect other people to fix your problems.

The quote you see above is one of the most stirring and inspirational ever uttered. JFK was asking his fellow Americans to ask what they as citizens could do for the greater good of their country. It was a time of turmoil in this country, but he knew that if Americans were tasked with contributing something to their society, they would be capable of extraordinary things.

Our society has changed since then, in some ways for the better and in many ways for the worse. Today, JFK's quote would be starkly different: "Ask not what you can do for your country, but what your country can do for you."

Personal responsibility is not as revered today as it once was. In fact, today, many Americans blame the government for not finding them a job, for not paying for their medical care, and for not sending them to college. Today's American is a radically different American from the one that watched a man land on the moon in 1969. That may seem like a long time ago, but it's just over forty years in a nation's history. Today, our institutions are designed to coddle and support. But few young people know the truth about the changes in our culture. Today's schools, and even today's parents, seem to have the attitude that their students need protecting from the truth about their government, their private institutions, and their educational system, all of which are failing them.

Our students today will be moving into the workforce at a time when our nation is in the midst of a dangerous transition. Our government is increasingly reckless with taxpayer dollars, and the endless credit (the money we borrow from other countries) we enjoyed as a superpower could dry up before we know it.

Finding your way in this world can be daunting. You probably have questions about a million things, starting with college, then likely moving on to career, family, living situation, and even your purpose in life. This book cannot answer all those questions directly, but it is meant as a primer on what you'll face as an American moving out into the "real world" beyond your days in school.

For as much you learn during your days in school, there is so much more you are not being told. After all, how much are you being taught about what it takes to run a business, about what taxes will mean for you and your family, about the current and proposed legislation of each major party and how it will affect you, and so on? Probably not very much.

You see, schools today focus mostly on theory and general knowledge. And that's good. You'll need to learn how you accumulate information and what interests you for the future and possible career choices. But there is a lot you need to know about your government and the people running it. What these people do will affect you for the rest of your life. The choices these people make in regard to taxes, immigration, federal spending, and the role of government may not seem particularly interesting right now. And why should they? Your teachers are probably repeating a version of history that has been edited and modified by big unions and big governments. And unless we know the truth about the mistakes made in history, we are doomed to repeat them.

In addition, even the pundits on TV seem to be talking to an audience much older than you are. They're talking to what they see as the "voting" public. Because until the election of 2008, most young people didn't vote. So they think, "Kids tend to worry about this stuff later, right?"

But now that the younger generation has taken part in the electoral process, and in large measure aided in the election of Barack Obama, it's time for these young people (that's you) to pay attention to what happens next. Will Barack Obama deliver on his promises of change? Will that change actually help our country, or are his policies changing who we are for the worst?

The assumption by many authors is that beyond these seminal political moments, kids aren't paying attention: that it was fun while it lasted but that young people will now revert to caring only for the social aspects of their lives. But we believe you and your peers care deeply about the issues of the world. We believe you are becoming more conscious every day about how the climate, the wars in Iraq and Afghanistan, the role of politics and even immigration are affecting your country. And even if you don't care that much right now, we are hoping this book will convince you to pay a little closer attention to what affects you and your family.

The reason? The people you see on television, in your classroom, and at political conventions are rarely telling you the entire truth about the way your country works, and especially the dire need to reverse some of the current policies moving our country closer to a place very different from what our founding fathers had in mind. Many just accept on face value the inherent "goodness" of what Barack Obama wants to change. He seems like such a charming man and supports so completely the Progressive agenda favored by mainstream media that few question his motives, his associations, or the goals he has for the nation.

Progressives: Progressives are liberals that want to move toward socialism or communism one step at a time, eventually progressing toward government control.

This book, however, is not entirely about President Obama. While his actions are certainly important to your future, there is a much larger government and many larger issues set to affect the way you live. And you're most likely ill prepared for them.

You aren't being taught what citizenship is about—the personal responsibility you have to your country to work hard, educate yourself, and become a productive person. You aren't being shown the nuts and bolts of immigration and what it is really costing our country. You aren't being told the truth about unions, business ownership, the motives of our politicians, and much, much more. And why not? Because many of the people in charge of teaching about this stuff are "in the bag." Teachers work for teachers unions; media members are overwhelmingly left-leaning, which means they are in favor of a big government. You see, the "left" is comprised of democrats who want the federal government to be involved in as much of our lives as possible. And in many cases, your parents or other mentors are unaware of the truth.

The United States of America is becoming a socialist state, a shadow of what it used to be and what made it great. Before you scoff at that statement, examine the evidence in this book and give it some time to soak in. Become an active student of our nation and its history and you'll see that the country you about to inherit is very, very different from the one your ancestors built through hard work.

Becoming an active citizen doesn't have to be hard either. Yes, the internet is a marvelous tool if you can trust the sources you're using. Learning how to be curious and vigilant is the hard part. As a student, you are no longer expected to develop an independent mind, to forage for yourself in a free market. You're expected to do what you need to pass, or not, and you'll be advanced through the grades with little hassle.

And when you finally do graduate, hard work will be more of an option. Slack off in school? No problem, the government will bail you out. If you get a low-paying menial job (or simply don't work), you'll pay fewer taxes (if any at all), you'll be given money to support your family, and you'll be paid for by someone who hasn't slacked off in life.

We hope to convince you to do otherwise. We hope that through this book you'll learn to work hard, to take control of your life, to pay attention to what's going on, and to take responsibility for your own actions. Before you decide which of these people you want to be, take a look at what this book has to offer. This is the "other side" of your education in politics, social policy, philosophy of government, immigration, and more. You'll learn about health care and other topics through stories you can relate to and in language that's easy to understand.

If you think these topics don't have anything to do with you, then think again. The world is fast becoming subject to a socialistic agenda supported even by the government and media of the United States. The individual is less important today than ever, and half of the nation's people don't contribute or create much of anything for the overall economy.

If you've ever thought about owning your own business, becoming an inventor, leading other people in a creative endeavor, or simply trying your best to be good at something, you're running headlong into a government that sees you as the enemy.

Right now you probably don't feel the urgency of what's being said here. But think back to the last time you participated in a sport or a competition where you had the chance to stand out. Did everyone get a trophy for participating? Did everyone get a certificate telling him or her how special his or her contributions were?

When everyone is coddled and treated as though he/she are truly special, then the individual efforts of each competitor are lost. If you beat the other team and the rewards for both sides are the same, then was winning really worth the effort? Couldn't you just show up, participate, and walk away a winner without ever trying your hardest? Winners are people who try their hardest and achieve their own personal goals, and there is no real winner if no one tries their hardest.

The same mentality that is stripping childhood games of real competition is also stripping the "grown-up" world of the incentive to work hard. The individuals that prepare their whole lives to conquer the career world are then told that their higher earnings will be taxed to pay for those who just participated. And this mentality is not limited to the economy.

Throughout the course of this book, we'll look at the following areas in order to understand just how much your future is being affected by government's and media's socialist leanings:

- Philosophy of government
- Personal responsibility
- Threats to the United States in the form of government, unions, advocacy groups, and illegal immigrants
- The divisiveness of ethnic loyalties
- Bailouts
- Health care
- Progressive Movement

We'll discuss our country as it stands now and how the government's failings in these many areas are punishing responsible Americans and encouraging a system where those who work hard and build careers are left supporting the bottom half of the citizenry—a group of people who may not work hard in school or who refuse to assimilate into American society.

While this book focuses on the many injustices and faults currently present in our economy, government, and health-care systems, it is ultimately a hopeful look of what could be if the individuals in the country were allowed to flourish. Our government plays a vital role in our lives, for better or for worse. If it were operated as intended by our founding fathers, we could once again enjoy the benefits of a truly free society. We believe we can once again become that America.

PART I

YOUR COUNTRY RIGHT NOW

History is a great teacher. It shows us the mistakes we've made, the triumphs we've earned, and the ways in which we as a people have evolved. But young people rarely bother to look back and usually spend even less time looking forward. Because of this "in the moment" attitude, it's easy for kids to miss the changes in our history that will one day negatively impact their lives.

Perhaps the biggest shift in our country has to do with personal responsibility. On the part of the average citizen and on the part of the government. You see, the average citizen faces several challenges to living the American dream as it were. There is the challenge of finding a good job as jobs are sent overseas. There is the challenge of staying qualified enough to justify your position at a company for the long term. And there is the challenge of overcoming crushing taxes and other legislative hurdles if you want to start your own business. But each of those problems is faced by a person actively engaged in trying to support himself or herself.

The larger problem is that not everyone is putting in this same effort. Not everyone is acting as responsibly. There is a relatively large portion of our society that has been reckless with their money, be they large institutions or private citizens. These people were faced with the consequences of their actions in 2008 when foreclosures exploded and bank failures dotted the landscape. Now there have always been people in our society who subsisted on handouts. I'm not talking about genuinely "in need" people here. These are people who never tried in school, who made no effort to support themselves and their families. And while we've always had people like these in our society, the problem is becoming worse because the government is doing more now than it ever has to support not only these people but also people who are firmly in the middle and upper class. If you are making efforts to excel in life, the government has saddled you with a burden before you've begun. It's like trying to win a race that you've trained for but having a weight placed around your neck just before the start of that race.

The government has spent more than $700 billion in the last year, giving handouts to failed businesses, private citizens in homes they can't afford, states on the verge of bankruptcy, and even to help developing nations battle climate change. This is money our nation does not have. That is something you need to really understand before we go any further. Our nation is supporting people in severe debt by going into really, really severe debt.

Our country does not have a warehouse full of cash. The federal government is like any private citizen in that it has to borrow money when it doesn't have the revenue it needs to pay for something. So it goes and borrows money from foreign countries looking to invest in U.S. treasuries. We'll talk about this more in a later chapter, but the point is that our country is handing out money it doesn't have in order to help people who spent money they didn't have. If you think that doesn't make sense, then you're right.

This overspending is much like the overspending private citizens do: it leads to massive debt, interest payments the government can't afford, and bad credit. This hasn't happened just yet, but our government has sent emissaries to China to try and convince them that we are not a credit risk. Think about that for a minute.

Our nation used to operate without a deficit. We made sure we spent only the money we had in our coffers. That has changed, and it is reflective of an attitude that shuns personal responsibility.

Our country is at a very important moment in time. We're changing as a people and as a nation, and these changes will affect your life, whether you want them to or not. You may not be thinking about the ways in which your government works or the impact media has in your life, but every day, your country is moving forward like a machine. The only question is whether or not you understand why the machine is going where it is and how you might be able to change its course.

There are a great many things affecting the course of our nation in this moment, and in each of the following chapters we'll try and explain how these things—socialist leanings, a biased media, lackluster schools, etc.—affect you and what you might do as an American citizen to make them better.

We'll begin in chapter 1 with government because it touches all of our lives in so many ways. The great thing about government though is that it can be changed and that its downward spiral is not irreversible.

CHAPTER 1

THE GOVERNMENT

The government of the United States was intended to be a citizen government. By that I mean that the citizens of the country were empowered to elect their own representatives and also to remove them from office peaceably. We aren't forced as Americans to overthrow the government through violence or to take up arms to defend ourselves from our representatives. We can, if we choose, campaign for their removal from office without fear of reprisal or imprisonment.

In return, our representatives are supposed to take care of the things we as private citizens couldn't be expected to provide on our own: paving of roads, police force, standing army, etc. Because we have full-time jobs and families to take care of, we cannot be expected to handle matters of national interest. The government that was designed by our founding fathers to address national issues was a pretty good one. Yes, it had its faults in that it recognized only white land owners as eligible to vote, but the overall premise was that the government would represent the needs of the people.

Our government was designed as a balanced system that favored the citizen and encouraged elected officials to avoid meddling too much in our lives. When our country was founded, there was no income tax, and the jobs the government put under its umbrella were far more limited than they are today. The number of social programs supported by the government and the wasteful spending of today's elected officials would boggle the mind our founding fathers.

What is happening now is a seismic shift in the way our elected officials govern the people. Private companies are being purchased by the government. Private individuals are being propped up by ever-increasing social programs, and the government is now poised to take over your medical care (if Barack

Obama gets his way). These actions are absolutely un-American. In fact, they are socialist.

We'll talk more about socialism in the next section, but for now, understand that our government has taken from its people the personal responsibilities that have kept us on track for hundreds of years. Instead of letting the public fail or succeed on their own merits in business, the government now acts as a major hand in the "free" market we once had.

The problem, of course, is that the more the government gets involved, the larger it gets. Large governments are inefficient. They are lumbering and laden with too many agendas and too much politicking. There's a reason why so little seems to get done in Washington, and that reason is size. The bigger a government (and the more people employed by it), the less likely it is to be in touch with the wants and needs of the people it is supposed to serve. And someone has to pay for this bigger government, and that someone is you!

As an example, look at the way in which most departments within the government are funded. The big "pot" of federal dollars (that would be your tax dollars) is massive. But it isn't so massive that there isn't competition for funding. You would think that a trillion-dollar budget would be enough to provide for everyone in this bloated government, but departments are constantly asking for more money.

Departments within our government are given an annual budget and told that their leftover money cannot carry over to the next year. They are "forced" to spend everything they are given, whether they need to or not. And each department knows that if they don't spend all the money they are given, they will be seen as needing less money the next year. And all the while they are telling the American people that they are striving to be as frugal as possible.

Your long-suffering parents are seeing their tax dollars squandered by a system that is so inefficient it slides billions of dollars further into debt *every day*. And instead of changing the system and encouraging real savings, the legislature is approving billions more in spending to push their way further into our lives.

If that sounds screwed up, that's because it is. It's like your parents leaving you in charge of how many texts you send during the month and giving you an unlimited budget to spend on said texts. What do you think the results would be? That's right, a phone bill the size of Kansas.

If you want a clear demonstration of how twisted current government operations are, just look at your local and state governments. These governments are not like private organizations. Private, for-profit organizations live and die by the bottom line. If they aren't making enough money, they have either to increase revenues or decrease costs, which can mean laying off workers, cutting back on operations, closing stores, etc.

The government, on the other hand, seems incapable of cutting costs. When was the last time you heard about a governmental body saying that they need less money? Have you ever heard of a cabinet member saying "No, we're good, thanks"? No. That's because the people in the government want their jobs and they want to keep working and building so that they can secure work for themselves. They don't care that their spending is costing the public billions and billions of dollars. And why should they? They have you and your parents. They simply increase taxes to pay their bills and, voilà, problem solved.

The People versus the Government

The citizens of the United States should run the government, not the other way around. That means that hardworking kids like yourself should be able to stand or fall on their own.

The government should not be running every aspect of your life, your health, your education, your retirement. But they will continue to do so until the people tell them to stop. Unfortunately, that kid in the corner who almost ruined your project is quite happy to be getting handouts. And he's not alone. There are millions of people just like him who will gladly vote for the politician who gave them a tax credit they didn't deserve.

So what can you do? First and foremost, you can vote for fiscally conservative politicians who will protect the government's coffers from overeager spenders. Vote! Your vote is your most direct means of communications with your elected representatives. If they're spending your parent's money to take care of people who won't take responsibility for their own lives, then vote them out of office.

Second, take care of yourself. Be a responsible person. Work hard in school, save your money, and pay off your student loans before you get the big-screen TV. The government will take 15 percent of everything you make and put it in this fund called social security because they don't believe you're going to save for your own retirement. And the fact that the system is almost broke means they're right that most people won't. The problem is that the government keeps taking more and more of your money. When social security was originally started by FDR, it was only 1 percent of your money, not 15 percent. On top of that, life expectancy has gone up, and now more and more people are receiving social security. Worse still, the government is stealing from social security to pay for other things. It was supposed to be in a secure fund where it could only be used for social security, and now the government can use that money for whatever it wants. And like many other government programs, this program is facing bankruptcy, so that means you cannot rely on the government for your retirement money even if that was their intention.

You can say "I'm going to take my own 15 percent out and do it myself." People don't realize that when they come out of school, they don't need to buy iPods and big-screen TVs. They don't realize that retirement and taxes have to come out first. You have to save 15 percent of your pay to go toward retirement. Spend another 5 percent to go toward disability and food, etc. You always have to save for retirement. That is part of your overhead as a person.

As soon as you start making money, set things up in a disciplined way. Fiscal responsibility is not taught in most schools, but it's the greatest service you can perform for your country. Don't become a burden on the social systems that were originally designed to help the truly needy. Your politicians are not going to stop spending, so stop spending for them.

Employers are matching a certain percentage of everything the government takes from you, and that burden will only become worse. Employers will fail more, and the government will buy them up through bailouts (which we'll discuss in a later chapter) and the socialist circle will just get tighter and tighter around us.

The liberal government is not in business to help other people; they are in business to help themselves. They're trying to keep in power by giving away entitlements. They don't care if they screw the 5 percent that have the money.

In order to really understand how badly the liberal government has skewed the public's view of taxes, consider this: *the top 5 percent of income earners pays 92 percent* of taxes in this country but is constantly treated as a villain. It's a classic divide-and-conquer, and it's working. Most Americans believe that the large corporation is the bad guy in our crumbling economy. They think that because these corporations earn billions of dollars, they must be evil. But those same corporations are employing your parents and your uncles and aunts and cousins.

So why do politicians constantly harass the top 5 percent for not paying their fair share? Because by causing class warfare, they can mobilize 95 percent of the people to get on their side and capture their votes. In a private company, if there was a select group of 5 percent of the people who paid for 92 percent of the company, they would be praised and highly represented in the company's decisions.

The Forever Politician

As long as politicians keep getting elected by "supporting the needy," they'll continue to do so. The problem is that they are not actually supporting the truly needy. They're supporting the needy and the lazy, and the truly needy are being painted with the same brush as the people who didn't work hard in school, won't hold down any job, and don't have a problem voting for a socialist government.

What this means is that the politicians screwing your parents are going to be screwing you. When you get into that good college and secure that solid career, you'll be faced with taxes that will astound you especially if you take the initiative to start your own business. You'll be punished for being successful and disciplined, and the money you lose will go the same place your parents' money is going.

The debate over limiting a politician's time in office through actual legislated term limits has been going on for years. Some say that it's necessary to avoid politicians being entrenched in their positions of power for term after term with little chance of being ousted. Others say that a new politician has little chance of passing meaningful legislation and that senior politicians are more experienced and better able to operate in Washington. So why haven't term limits ever been instituted, and are they a good thing?

They haven't been instituted because the people who would need to pass term-limit legislation are the same ones who would be thrown out of office by term limits. George Washington, founding father, stepped down after his term to demonstrate the ethics of our political system. Government's intentions from helping the people to helping themselves has clearly changed.

Asking a career politician to throw himself or herself out of office is like asking prisoners to police themselves. Now as to whether or not they are a good thing: the answer is yes. And here's why. Career politicians are motivated by one thing only: getting reelected. They want to keep their jobs. After all, being a United States senator is a pretty cushy gig. You're treated as what you are: a power politician with a lot of influence. You get a great salary, and you have tremendous influence over public policy. Who would want to leave that job?

Elected officials may show up in Washington with the hopes that they can make a difference. And many do. But once they arrive, they realize quickly that in order to get reelected they need to show the people of their district that they are, in fact, doing something on their behalf. The easiest way to do this for a junior politician is to get a piece of the pork barrel: federal money used for local projects. But in order to secure these funds, they usually have to do favors for a more senior politician, one with more sway. That means supporting legislation they may or may not agree with.

Washington is a little bit like the lunchroom in middle school: the politicians are looking for a better lunch, and so they barter with their neighbors in order to get what they want. Don't want Mom's mashed potatoes? Well, it turns out your neighbor wants some mashed potatoes and he has a brownie he's willing to trade. And so it goes in Washington, the major difference being that instead of exchanging small food items, they're exchanging billions of dollars in tax money. And that really is the crux of the problem with politicians who decide to stay forever. They forget whose money they're spending, and they lose sight of just how much it is they're wasting.

The easiest thing in the world is to spend other people's money. With politicians knowing they can stay in office for as long as they keep getting reelected, there is little incentive to do anything *but* spend the money, and fast. Constituents like having money lavished on their districts. It's nice to have good roads and new buildings and monuments paid for by the federal government. And if your politicians keep you in the money, you'll likely keep reelecting them. But this approach is doomed to failure.

Rarely do politicians make it their first priority to reduce spending or to ensure that there is a surplus in the federal budget. They don't act as you or I have to act when we budget for ourselves. We have to pay down our debts and save for "rainy days," but they don't bother. Paying down the trillions of dollars in debt? That's someone else's problem. Saving for a rainy day? They can always claim it's raining right now in order to justify more spending.

Of course, when it's one politician acting this way, it's bad enough. Now multiply this kind of behavior by the number of people in the House and Senate, and you will see why the government is so wasteful. It's like being in a relationship with hundreds of people who have a spending addiction and a virtually unlimited budget.

It is so easy to spend money that you don't directly have to work for. These people do not have to work any harder to spend one dollar than they do to spend a billion dollars (which would be nice in our private lives). If you were running a school club and you had to generate all of your own spending money, you would be a lot more careful how you spent it than if money were given to you by the PTA or by the school.

Now consider you are a member of the House of Representatives. You have to be elected every two years, which means you are basically campaigning for your next election as soon as you are put into office. Now let's say that you have a great idea for a bill that is truly needed but will cost millions of dollars.

In order to get your important bill passed, you will need the support of all the other elected officials in the Congress. Each one of these supporters requires a special addition to satisfy their needs, and when you multiply that by 435 members of the House and one hundred members of the Senate, that simple bill explodes into a billion-dollar piece of legislature. This is called pork barrel, when each politician gets to add something to a bill in exchange for a promise that he or she will vote to pass the bill.

Socialism on the rise

All these outrageous expenditures—encouraged and approved by President Barack Obama—are pushing the government away from the lean necessity-providing entity it was designed to be and into socialist territory. In case you aren't familiar with socialism, it means the government, or "state," owns everything and "provides" the people with what they need. It's as though the government has decided to become everyone's parent.

Of course, because large governments are so inefficient, their efforts to operate private industries are disastrous. The systems become cumbersome because they're no longer based on profits, and the services provided to you become worse and worse and worse. And if these "government companies" aren't profitable, they have a seemingly unlimited amount of money to help prop them up—your money.

Even more disturbing is that as we slide toward socialism, the individual—the very basis of our nation—is being drowned out. You and your classmates are becoming anonymous faces in a machine that cares little about who works hard, who excels, and who cares enough about their own futures to do something positive.

That kid that sits beside you that spends chemistry class picking his nose is going to be propped up by the government when he inevitably fails to find solid work. Without work, he won't have enough money to support a family, even though he'll probably start one. All the while you'll be paying for him to do nothing, and should he decide to have ten kids while he's unemployed, you'll be supporting them too.

Welfare programs for the needy are a worthy use of government services. Not everyone who loses their home or their job is a lazy bum. It's good that the government has seen fit to help people in a time of need. But these programs are allowing certain people to go on indefinitely without real improvement in their work ethic, job skills, or self-sufficiency. And that holds true for all races and religions.

So why the push toward socialism? What does the governing class get out of it? Well, they get to keep their jobs. In exchange for handing out freebies to a huge swath of the public, they earn votes, which keep them in office and living a life of luxury and privilege. Politicians are often railed against because they take the money of lobbying firms and wealthy businessmen. They are accused of catering to a small percentage of the populace at the expense of the many. But that's backward.

These "few" are the wealthy, the ones paying a huge percentage of the taxes the government squanders every year. They have worked hard to build industries and businesses, and they deserve to be heard. They deserve to keep more of their hard-earned money and to not have it thrown down the drain in a socialist system of government handouts.

I'm sure at some point that you've been paired up with other kids in your classes for the sake of completing large projects. Inevitably you've been thrown into a group with a few hardworking students and a few who do nothing at all. But instead of each student getting an individual assessment of his or her efforts, the entire group shares on grade. The kid that sat in the corner doing nothing is sharing your A! And for what? If everyone were graded on their individual work, everyone would try harder, and the final project would be a much better project.

CHAPTER 2

BARACK OBAMA IS NOT GOOD
FOR THE YOUTH OF AMERICA

Barack Obama won the presidential election promising to fundamentally transform America. What was his grand plan? Nobody really seemed to know. Most people were so caught up in the media's anti-Bush propaganda they didn't pay attention to the details of what Mr. Obama was saying. It didn't matter . . . they wanted a change.

People were so used to hearing about the "last eight years" they forgot that Mr. Bush had inherited a falling economy and that for six years of his presidency the economy was prosperous. They forgot that the Congress had a Democratic majority in the last two years of his administration. But in one sense, Obama has a point. It doesn't matter who is in power, Democratic or Republican; the economy of the United States cannot prosper unless we do have a *fundamental change* in the way the government is run.

The problem lies with Mr. Obama's vision of change. It is 180 degrees away from helping. It's like trying to fly from Los Angeles to New York by heading north. Yes, we need a change, but heading due west is not the change we need. You will find yourself lost and desperate and way worse off than you were. Let's explain and show you the correct path.

The government takes care of the elderly with social security and Medicare. These are huge "entitlements" that the government has promised us. Sounds nice. This way, my family does not have to worry about taking care of me when I can no longer work, and not only that, but I don't have to worry about saving for retirement because the government will do that for me. Instead of me saving 15 percent of my paycheck toward retirement and putting it in investments of my choosing, the government will take money from me and an equal amount from my employer and save it for me until I retire (about age sixty-two). Not only forcing me to save but forcing my employer had to pay for me too. Sounds like the government has my back!

Now with a robust population working and forced saving for the future, a tremendous amount of money pours into the federal government's hands. And this money doesn't have to be spent now. It is for later. So the money piles up. We all know what happens when we have a big pile of cash just sitting there in front of us with few restrictions on its expenditure. We look to our right and we have bills to pay; we look to our left and there is a stack of Benjamins that nobody needs right now . . . that's tempting, but it isn't really our money. We are trusted to save that money for when people get older. So retirement money is in the hands of our "daddy," the government, because he knows that we are too stupid and impetuous to save it or invest it.

But Daddy has bills (not to mention he has to pay more government workers—the Social Security Administration to look after us—using more government money), so the government decided it is okay to use our retirement money for other stuff. Well, now that the fastest-growing segment of our population is in their retirement years and fewer people are working, we have a problem.

Back in the "unenlightened" smaller-government days, most people had four or more children who would share the burden of taking care of their parents (with no administrative costs) in their retirements. But now people have fewer children to take care of them. Each child is forced to pay more of their own paycheck to support their parents. Let's say you have no children; someone else's child will have to pay for you. That is exactly what is happening now.

The government has spent the sacred retirement savings. They decided it is okay to use your parents' savings. So they rely on new payments (intended for use decades from now) to pay the retirement costs of current retirees. There is no time for the money to accumulate interest, and so now we're looking at a future that seems to hold nothing for your retirement. You will be paying for parents and grandparents that you don't even know, but the government owes them.

You are the government, so you owe them. So you better hope the growth rate of the working force increases fast, or you will never see any of your contribution. Unfortunately, our country's population is top-heavy, meaning more retirees than workers. *Maybe we will just have the government control health care so that we can ration it from the older people and they will die off quicker . . . no, that could never happen in the United States . . . unless there is a fundamental change.*

So the inefficient big government and its bankrupted entitlement plans have not worked out so well. Perhaps that is why our founding fathers wanted a small federal government, and people were forced to be responsible for their own families. That brings us back to our pilot from LA to New York, Mr. Obama.

Surely he will fundamentally change the system, right? Oh yeah, he is turning the plane west over the ocean. His plan is bigger government! Can you believe that? Who pays for the government? You do. He wants more borrowing (you personally already owe $350,000) but calls it a stimulus bill. He adds yet more borrowing and calls it a jobs bill (*people get tired of hearing about taking on more debt, so he calls it a stimulus bill or jobs bill*). Not to mention, the government under Obama is trying to control the banks, the auto industry, and now health care.

President Obama's administration will give more of your money away just to get these bills passed. If the senator for Louisiana doesn't want the health-care bill, we will bribe her with $300 million!!! After all, it is not the president's money, it is your money. And this is just a peek into this "fundamental change" he's offered.

The president and his cabinet have almost no experience in the private sector. He has the all-time lowest percentage of advisors who have private-sector experience. That is not an accident. He picks them deliberately. But what does that mean? It means his philosophy is one of government controlling everything because he believes the citizenry are too stupid and to take care of themselves (*you now know the government is far worse*).

It means that the source of a paycheck for his advisers has been tax collection. They did not earn their money. They do not have to hire people to generate income, and if they gamble and waste the money they do have, it doesn't hurt their pocketbooks at all. So now we have an administration whose only experience with money is to spend the piles of it that people have worked their collective backsides off for (and are required to give to feed this bottomless pit of spending). So it means nothing to them to give a billion dollars here or $784 billion there or billions in bribes (called earmarks) to get bills passed.

The president has stated many times that he is a Progressive. Let there be no doubt; he says it himself. A Progressive is not really a Democrat (which explains why he has had to bribe so many Democrats to get spending bills passed), he is an über-Democrat. A Progressive (*kinder, gentler term for socialist or communist—kinda like* chubby *is for fat people*) believes in big government *controlling* your life. It doesn't matter that Progressive ideas have never worked to create a thriving economy; the president will stay the course 180 degrees away from the target because that is what he believes, that is what he knows, and that is what the people he picks to be his associates believe.

He will do whatever it takes to change America from a country where individual people are strong, productive, hardworking, innovative, and self-reliant to one where people are utterly dependent on government. He thinks he and his so-called elite friends not only know what is best but also that they can provide what is best to you. We know that the inefficient big government cannot take your money from you and give it back to you (or whomever they decide needs it more than you do) more efficiently than you can spend your own money.

Pieces of your money get siphoned off into several government agencies before they make their way back to you (or whomever they choose to give it to). Are we on planet backward? Is it so simple to see what is right that maybe we are missing something that only a few wise men can see and we are supposed to trust them?

No. Mr. Obama wants to level the playing field, to give all the D and E students Cs and all the A and B students Cs. After all, the A and B students have had it too good. Continuing with the educational theme, if you just give him your 90s and 100s, he will give those grades to the students getting the 50s and 60s so that we can all live in beautiful harmony. He wants to "redistribute the wealth."

President Obama does not pay attention to the facts. He does not operate in the real world. He is a progressive ideologue. He wants a big government and powerful unions. You and I know unions do not create products or exports or jobs. Unions redistribute power from the companies to the workers. They level the playing field. Does this theme sound familiar? Workers have come a long way since the "sweat shops," poor pay, and dangerous factory conditions at the turn of the century—thanks to the early unions. Now we have government agencies like OSHA (Occupational Safety and Health Administration) that enforce safety at the workplace. We have a federal minimum wage.

So the unions find themselves struggling for purpose. So they often strong-arm company employees to join the unions. Remember, unions do not produce anything to sell; they are dependent on member's dues payments (just like the government is on tax dollars) for their existence. Unions go to successful companies that are currently not using union workers and try to get the workers to become part of the union. Workers typically cast a private vote on whether or not to join.

Imagine if your class was voting on whether or not to let five new bullies join the SGA. They are in the room while you vote. There are two options to cast your vote. One is anonymously on a folded piece of paper collected in a closed box, and the other is by raising your hand. The anonymous vote ensures privacy and keeps you safe from intimidation and retaliation. That is the way presidential elections are run (you go behind a private curtain or cubicle).

If you were forced to raise your hand in order to vote, everyone would see you raise your hand. Everyone would know your name and where you live. Obama wants nonunion employees to have to raise their hand. He wants to remove the secret ballot, thus creating more "fundamental" change. Thanks, Mr. Obama and friends.

Unions use strikes to force bargaining over contract changes. In many the union contracts make it almost impossible to fire a union employee. So many nonproductive people are getting paid to do less work than other people might. If you own a business, does that seem fair? Union workers also get a more lucrative benefits package than many nonunion workers do. That sounds great on the surface, but there is a problem: the cost of a union worker is higher, so the company often has to charge more money for its products and services.

Now that we have a global-based economy, we can go to other countries to hire less-expensive employees. Makes sense. The company cannot compete on price with local employees, so fire them and move the plant to Mexico or buy from China and the Philippines, where labor is cheaper. The rest of the world will not spend more for your products and services when they can buy from China, for example. So you either close the company or go with foreign workers.

When unions have gotten in the middle, between the members and the companies that hire and produce, the members lose. They create an adversarial atmosphere so that you have the company and its best interests on one side and the employees and their best interests on the other side. Why do you think we have lost so many factories and jobs in this country? (*By the way, that means less people to pay the entitlements that have already been promised.*)

Why do politicians appease the unions as jobs are circling the drain in this country?

Because unions influence how their members vote. So if you are running for homecoming king or queen and the representatives from each class said they could deliver most of the votes in their respective grades if you did one thing for them, you would do what they wanted in order to get elected, even if that thing may not be ethical. Your choice would be to let the "block votes" go to your opponent or to take the easy way out.

That is how politicians get elected. They do what is necessary to get the teachers unions, the labor unions, and the law enforcement unions on their sides. In fact, our president actually consults union leaders before making changes.

He has said it himself. The person who visited the White House most often in the first six months of this administration was union leader Andy Stern. Let's see; we have two wars, a soon-to-be-nuclear Iran, terrorist plots, a struggling economy, and $100 trillion in liabilities; but Mr. Obama meets most often with a union leader. Where do you think his priorities really are? Oh yeah, fundamental change.

When Obama was elected in November 2008 as the forty-fourth president of the United States of America, many believed that that the nation would be turning the page on its long history of racist behavior. And with his election, we did take a measurable step toward overcoming some of that legacy. But that does not mean Barack Obama is going to help get our country back on track, either financially or politically.

The Democratic Party is now in control of both houses of the national legislature, the House of Representatives and the Senate. They tout their health-care legislation as being tough on insurance companies and guaranteeing coverage for everyone, even if they have a preexisting condition or are old. What they didn't tell the public was that insurance companies would still be able to charge these people exorbitant fees.

As we've stated before in this book, the government is grossly inefficient and incapable of running any program at a cost that can compete with private industry. So why would Barack Obama, a man who claims to be a pragmatist, support the legislation? Because he believes firmly in socialist ideals, even if he says he is in no way a socialist.

First, let's begin with a bit of a history lesson. What is socialism, and where did it come from? Well, the *American Heritage Dictionary* defines it as "any of various theories or systems of social organization in which the means of producing and distributing goods is owned collectively or by a centralized government that often plans and controls the economy." If that sounds familiar, then you're right on track. For the past year, under Barack Obama's leadership, the government has been buying up stakes in several of our nation's largest companies: GM, Citigroup, AIG, and many others of the nation's largest banks. Our government bought $250 billion of stock in struggling banks as part of the $700 billion TARP bailout package. If that isn't socialism, I don't know what is.

Now supporters of Obama will claim that the TARP program was started in President George W. Bush and that President Obama is merely continuing the program. But he has done much more than just continue the program. Under his leadership, the Democrat-controlled Senate and House of Representatives have poured billions more into programs such as Cash for Clunkers, foreclosure reform, and other programs that put the government in direct involvement in what is supposed to be a capitalist economy.

There is no doubt that these actions can easily be veiled under the guise of "emergency" stimulus, that without it our economy would crumble and we would be in the midst of another Great Depression. But the fact remains that our government now owns a large portion of business across the nation. And they haven't stopped there.

Now Barack Obama has a direct hand in your health care, your insurance, your student loans, your mortgage. He has a hand in everything, and that is socialist by any definition. Why does Obama want these things?

The youth of America overwhelmingly supported President Obama. He is charismatic, a great orator, young, dynamic, and a man great at making grand promises. Who doesn't want change for the better? Who doesn't want Washington shaken up, and who doesn't want to be told that "yes, we can" live a better life and build a better future. But those catchy phrases and easy promises provide little in the way of specifics. It's easy to get caught up in rhetoric when you're young. You want to be told that your future is going to be better than what your parents are living. You want to know that you'll have a job and good health care and that you'll be able to live the American dream. It's only when you're a bit older that you learn to be more cautious, that you realize that the American dream can't be provided for by the president or any other politician.

If you're a fan of President Obama's, you may be looking at what I'm saying and dismissing it out of hand. After all, a lot of crazies have attacked President Obama and accused him of being everything from a Muslim terrorist to a stooge for radical leftist groups. It's easy to dismiss any critic of the president as being another voice in the crowd. But saying the president is socialist is not an unfounded rumor or an accusation that has no merit.

If you have nothing to fear by examining the president's record, then discussing in detail his actions as a politician and community activist shouldn't be an issue. And when you do look closely, what you find is a man who strongly believes in government intervention and ownership by the "people" of much of our most important infrastructure. His actions and his policies speak volumes, and were he to be described to you as a foreign politician, you would immediately say that he fits the description of a socialist as defined in the dictionary.

The socialist president of Venezuela remarked during climate talks in Copenhagen, Denmark, in 2009 that President Obama had "just nationalized nothing more and nothing less than General Motors. Comrade Obama! Fidel, careful or we are going to end up to his right." It was a statement that came from a seeming madman, a man dismissed by most as crazy or dangerous or both. Chávez has nationalized his nation's oil reserves and knows better than most do when he sees a fellow socialist. He knows what it means to take control of the power and wealth bases of your country under the guise of making life better for the "little guy."

One of socialism's main tenets is that capitalism serves only the very highest earners and that it is inefficient because these people want only to take care of themselves, that they care little for the average person and so make little effort to improve societal systems. The answer, of course, is to give the worker ownership of the products he produces. To take the wealth from a small group of "evil" capitalists in order to distribute it to the disadvantaged worker who gives his blood, sweat, and tears to creating that wealth.

Obama has proposed doing exactly that. In order to gain support for his health-care reform and his other programs, he proposed increasing taxes on the very wealthy, meaning families that earn more than $250,000 a year, a number which is decreasing. Let's look at that objectively and see what that implies.

These wealthy people have earned their money by creating wealth for others through the building of companies that provide jobs to millions. They have earned their wealth by having skills, vision, entrepreneurialism, and drive that others have not had. They have often spent their lifetimes building their wealth, and they are above all private citizens living by the same laws as other people do. President Obama is proposing taking more of their money in order to provide for the "less fortunate" or the people, as a socialist might say.

If you look at his proposals in black-and-white terms, you get socialism. Chavez nationalized all of the industry in his nation, just as François Mitterrand did in France. They took ownership of industrial conglomerates because they believed that these enterprises were corrupted by capitalism and the greed that fed their massive profits. Well, look at how Obama has described the people running the companies his government is taking control of: he called the bankers on Wall Street "fat cats" and said he didn't intend to see the bailout money simply aid them.

Again, his words reflect a strong belief in corralling "out of control" capitalists in order to save the people. That is exactly what Chavez has done and what Mitterrand did in France. Just because it is happening in a supposedly capitalist society does not mean it isn't happening. It is; just look objectively, and you'll see that.

It is no different than teachers using the highest score in the class to establish a sliding scale for grades. For example, you work hard, you study what you're supposed to learn, and you get a 95. But nobody else in the class got even close to that score. Some teachers will throw out any outliers like yours and use the class average to establish a grading scale. If the next highest score was 70, then that is called an A, and everything below is adjusted accordingly. Does that sound fair? It sounds good too at the time, but just think; now everyone will try less assuming that that grading curve will always be there for them. And the overall knowledge level of the class will go down.

President Obama says a lot of things that sound good. He says he'll control greed on Wall Street, but then he hires former Goldman Sachs employees to reform Wall Street. He says he'll get us out of the wars in Iraq and Afghanistan in a responsible manner, and then he escalates the war in Afghanistan, saying that we as a nation have a responsibility to defend ourselves against the evil in the world. Sound familiar? It ought to: his language sounds remarkably like that of President George W. Bush, another big spender.

President Obama may indeed turn out to be for change, but it won't be change we can believe in. Eventually, someone has to pay the tab. Our country will one day soon be faced with a bill so large it will make your head spin. Just like the college freshman who spends money he doesn't have, reality will be harsh for the Americans forced to pay off the trillions of dollars our government is spending.

There is old expression used to describe someone who is shortsighted, and it goes, "Penny wise and pound foolish." It relates to English currency, the pound, and it basically means that someone is so focused on small, short-term problems that they overlook the big picture.

By no means is the current economic crisis a small problem, but President Obama is still being "pound foolish." Let us assume that his bailout works to revive the economy. Let us assume that his health-care plan passes in some form. And now let us assume that these legislative money pits somehow revive the American economy. The money spent to accomplish this feat will mean the entire process was not worth the trouble.

The fact is that no amount of government spending can revive the economy on its own. The economy recovers when all the Americans who were laid off (and their neighbors, who are afraid of being laid off) regain their jobs and find secure financial footing. Our economy runs on confidence, and consumers don't all of a sudden forget their anxieties because the government is pouring billions of dollars into big banks and collapsing carmakers. But still the government spends.

So let us now fast-forward twenty years. You are in the midst of your career as an engineer and hoping to start your own consulting firm. You excel at your work and you are on the fast track to being a respected expert in your field. You want to capitalize on that, and so you get together with a few colleagues and start your firm. It's a huge success, and the money starts coming in. And then you get hit with a massive income tax, a payroll tax, and you are required to provide health care for all your employees at massive expense. Then you are told that in the next two years your taxes will be climbing even higher because a new social program has been created by the government. They are taxing successful business owners such as yourself to pay for the program.

That's the future envisioned by Barack Obama. It's a future that has no place for successful, hardworking Americans who have the audacity to think they can keep some of the money they work so hard to earn.

CHAPTER 3

THE ECONOMY

Watch the pennies and the dollars will take care of themselves.
—Benjamin Franklin

The economy. Today you can't go to a news Web site, news station, Twitter feed, or blog without someone talking about the economy. Everyone is talking about how bad the economy is and who's to blame. After all, we haven't seen this kind of economic collapse since the Great Depression. There are a lot of people providing their opinions on what should be done and especially who is to blame. Some people blame the big banks, others blame people who bought homes they couldn't afford, and still others blame the government for not regulating the financial industry as tightly as it should have.

Fixing the economy is not going to be easy. There are many, many things wrong with it, and the housing crisis is far from over. You most likely know someone who lost their home or who at least had trouble paying their mortgage every month probably because they were laid off. Everyone seems to have an opinion on what should be done, and there is a lot of noise surrounding this issue right now. As a student, you probably only see or hear what's on the news or what is happening to your parents or your town. But there is more to this situation than meets the eye.

In times of crisis, it's common for people to want drastic change, to believe that whatever happened was the result of massive flaws in the system. These same people want steps taken to ensure that a collapse of this magnitude never happens again. And in order to fix these problems, they want the government to step in and take control over private industries to make sure that greedy barons aren't stealing the public's money. And in order to help those that were harmed by the collapse, they want the government to guarantee jobs, to secure faulty mortgages, and to bail out anyone and everyone that might be in financial trouble.

But let's think about that attitude for just a minute. If you believe that the economy is in trouble because the banks were careless with their money and that people shouldn't have been spending money they didn't have, you're probably smart enough to figure out that the government shouldn't do those same things in order to "fix" the economy. Why should the government borrow tens of billions of dollars that it can't pay back anytime soon in order to invest it faulty banks or in jobs programs that may or may not work? Shouldn't the government be working to secure your tax dollars in ways that are superior to what your banks did with your deposits?

Why should the government be taking risks with money? Granted, the government is in a position to help people when they are in hard times, but there are limits to what can and should be done. So why has the government been so quick to dole out the dollars?

Well, the answer is pretty simple, actually; it's about votes. Very few people are going to look poorly upon a helping hand. As I said in the previous chapter, the government's job is to protect its citizens from circumstances beyond their control, and most people are grateful to any administration that has shown them personal attention in the form of a direct handout. And besides, isn't it the right thing to do? The low-level workers in a large institution have very little control over whether or not their company makes stupid investment decisions. Should they be laid off or furloughed, the government can do a lot of good by providing some financial support and even job training. In most cases, yes. But there's more to our economy than just the low-level worker.

As stated earlier, our economy is in the shape it's in because of stupid financial decisions on the part of both the private citizen and the private institution. During the real estate boom, people were spending money they borrowed at ridiculous terms, all in the hope that they could skip over earning their way up to a comfortable living. And private institutions were doing anything and everything they could to take advantage of that spending frenzy. And that's a natural part of our economy, one that should be left alone.

In past years, prior to the real estate bubble, when a person applied for a mortgage, they had to prove that they had the means to pay it back. It wasn't a handout; it was a loan. Before the banks lent money, they used to verify your income and any assets that you may have had. Then in the 1970s, the government saw that minorities were not getting as many loans as nonminorities were, so the brilliant government stepped in. The government said to the banks, "You must give out loans to more minorities, even if they cannot prove that they will be able to pay them back."

Naturally, the banks were reluctant to do so because it makes no business sense, but the government said that they had entities that would buy their loans from them to protect them from losses. Those entities were Fannie Mae and Freddie Mac. But when people who couldn't afford the houses in the first place could not make the payments, they walked away. Many times they did not put any money into the houses to begin with (no money-down loans), so they had nothing to lose.

Fannie Mae and Freddie Mac would package individual loans into groups and sell them to Wall Street investors who would collect the interest payments from the loans. To make these packages more attractive to investors, many were insured by companies like AIG. With government involvement, people who couldn't pay their loans walked away from them. This caused the collapsing of banks, Fannie Mae and Freddie Mac, Wall Street, and AIG. But don't worry; the government is back in offering your tax money as a bailout for these companies. Now you are the backstop for all these bad decisions. Unfortunately, the government has to borrow the money, and now you are also on the hook for all of the interest payments on that money.

The economy in the United States has experienced multiple booms and busts, most notably in 1929, at the beginning of the Great Depression. This recession has not proven to be as bad, but some of the same forces that caused the Depression of 1929 to become the Great Depression can be blamed for today's economic mess, namely big government spending and entitlement programs.

Personal responsibility used to be a cornerstone of American living. The independent, hardy frontier families could depend only on themselves for success, and they were the only ones to blame when things went wrong. But things have changed drastically in this country. Today, if a family buys a home they can't afford, they don't pay the same price as they used to. Instead of being evicted, the government has stepped in to make foreclosure proceedings harder for the lenders. What's more, many families are simply walking away from their homes, taking the ten-year hit on their credit and the embarrassment of having stretched their budgets too far.

Surely, these families are suffering humiliation. No one wants to be foreclosed on or sent packing with nowhere to go. Many of these families, however, have no one to blame but themselves. Which is also true for the many financial institutions which peddled financial products based on these extremely risky home purchases. The men and women working in these banks and investment firms wanted nothing more than to make a quick buck. And many of them did—millions of bucks, in fact. And when they went bust? You guessed it; the government stepped in once again to save the day.

By intervening, the government is masking the true state of the economy. Instead of allowing these irresponsible large institutions to fail, the government has propped them up, leading many to wonder if the bailouts are simply delaying the inevitable collapse of one or many large banks.

False economic support lends uncertainty and doubt to the economic climate in this country. If you took a test in school and your teacher announced that any student who had failed the test would be given a good grade, just temporarily, until they could study some more, you'd be pissed. You worked hard, and now others are getting free rewards. That would make your circumstances uncertain. You would doubt the validity of a system that is supposed to reward those who make the right decisions and who work hard.

The same can be said for our economy today. People are beginning to doubt whether or not the hardworking, innovative minds in this country have any real incentive to create something new. They can be taken down by a redistribution of wealth, by other institutions that have acted foolishly, or by overregulation by the government.

This three-pronged attack on industry survivors is troubling. The bailouts are creating government-owned businesses that have no incentive to clean up their acts. And with these businesses "polluting" the business climate, no one is sure what the future will bring. Will they eventually collapse again, dragging other healthy businesses down? Will they make investors of all stripes skittish, even when the economy begins to recover? How can a company convince people to invest in it when they do business with organizations that were bailed out?

A Home for Everyone!

There was a time when purchasing a home was a major event in someone's life. It required a lot of advanced saving and planning, and it was difficult to get approved by a bank for a mortgage. Most banks required that applicants had 20 percent to put down on their home purchase (a huge amount compared to today's standards), and it was understood that not everyone would be able to meet these terms. Not everyone could by a house.

The problem, of course, is that liberals couldn't stand the idea of millions of Americans living without their own homes. After all, America is about equality, and that means everyone should have the American dream of a home and white picket fence. But America was never designed to ensure that everyone had everything.

That's why it's a free-market economy. Giving everyone the same things means adopting socialism. In America, you have to earn the things you want.

Regardless of what was right, Progressive liberals got legislation passed to ease the standards for lending and to essentially force banks to lend to people who had less-than-desirable credit scores. These changes were made under the guise of helping more minorities into homes, but how does it help an American of any color to put them into a home they can't afford?

Everyone wants to live the American dream, but rushing that dream and forcing the market to act in ways that aren't sensible can ruin it quickly. That is what Democrats did, and the results were predictable: the thousands and thousands of Americans in homes they couldn't afford stopped paying their mortgages. They are in over their heads, and now the rest of the country is paying for it through out-of-control spending in the form of bailouts.

And whom is the government bailing out? Fannie Mae and Freddie Mac, the two private entities tasked with backing up many of these risky mortgages. And to AIG, one of the insurance companies that insured the financial instruments created to trade and sell these mortgages. It has cost the government billions upon billions of dollars to clean up this mistake, and their efforts to clean it up haven't worked. The housing market is still in shambles, and millions of Americans are finding out that the American dream done wrong can be a nightmare.

Cash for Clunkers

A good example of a government initiative designed to boost the economy is the Cash for Clunkers program which saw hundreds of thousands of Americans receive as much as $4,500 in government subsidies in return for buying a new more fuel-efficient car. The program was originally given $1 billion, the idea being that this money would help to clear the lots of car dealers while also putting "greener" cars on the roads for America. Of course, being a government program, it went wrong.

You see, some Americans saw the program for the disaster it was. They realized that junking thousands of still-usable automobiles would be anything but "green." They also realized that the government is a naturally wasteful entity and the participation in the program would mean supporting spending that we as a nation could not afford. Others though were blinded by the specter of "free" money and jumped at the chance. In fact, too many people jumped at the chance, and an additional $2 billion was spent on the program when it ran out of money months ahead of when it was supposed to end.

This program, like so many other socialist programs put forward by the Democratic leadership in America and unfortunately supported by many conservatives as well, was a disaster. If you know anything about history, you know that accepting the government's money when you don't need it is a simply adding to the problems our nation faces as it stares down a huge deficit.

The American taxpayer ended up spending much more than the $4,500 per vehicle intended under the program (which paid out smaller amounts for less fuel-efficient trucks and SUVs). In fact, the American taxpayer doled out about $24,000 per vehicle according to a study by Edmunds.com, an automotive research and reporting Web site.

You see, the Cash for Clunkers authorities claimed that there were 690,000 vehicles sold as a result of the program. But Edmunds.com found that only 125,000 of the vehicles sold could be attributed directly to the program. They found that the rest of the vehicles sold would have been purchased anyway.

Sales of cars would have gone up anyways because the average price of a car at the time of the program was relatively low, at $26,915 with an average cash rebate of $1,667, reducing that price even further. Americans were ready to take advantage of fantastic deals the automakers were offering. The government stepped in and said, "We'll help, but there are rules for receiving our money."

When purchasing a car under the program, a buyer had to fill out more forms than you'd likely see when purchasing a house. There were forms certifying that each household was only using the program to purchase one car. There were forms certifying that the vehicle being traded in was less fuel-efficient than the car being purchased. There were forms certifying that if the government deemed the purchase to not match their criteria, the car purchaser would be responsible for repaying the dealer the $4,500 they were owed.

And of course, the government didn't provide money up front for dealerships to dole out. In fact, dealerships had to borrow millions of dollars in advance to cover the cost of providing the rebates themselves. Then they had to apply for reimbursement from the government.

In the end, the program produced tons and tons of extra paperwork (not very green) and added hours to the purchase of each vehicle. And if Edmunds. com's numbers are correct, we as taxpayers spend about $24,000 per vehicle that can be directly attributed to the program. If you think about those numbers, it's shocking. The owners of these new vehicles are paying tens of thousands of dollars for them, and the dealers did indeed experience a huge boost in sales. But now the rest of America's taxpayers have been dragged into the process and at a rate that is simply outrageous.

Did anybody really save any money? By the time our government pays off the $3 billion it spent on the program, including interest, did anybody come out ahead? If you look at the $24,000 the taxpayers were putting out for each vehicle and add that to the cost paid for each vehicle by the new owners, you have vehicles costing us as Americans twice what they are worth. How is that stimulus?

And we as taxpayers are not without blame for this. When you look at the government as your baby daddy as so many Americans do, you just contribute to their wasteful spending. If Americans had stood up and said, "We'll buy cars when we're ready. Save my tax dollars and put it toward paying off the deficit," we'd be much better off as a nation.

The Cash for Clunkers Program, technically called the Car Allowance Rebate System, or CARS (you see, the government likes clever acronyms), is indicative of how freely our government is spending our tax dollars. And in fact they are spending more than our tax dollars. They are spending the money we give them and then borrowing billions more to fund programs like this one. It's a waste and a quick way to bury our country under a mountain of debt we might never be able to overcome.

Health Care

If these government-owned zombie institutions aren't bad enough, business leaders and private citizens have to deal with another troubling trend: health care. The government claims that evil corporations, both pharmaceutical and insurance, are squeezing the little guy out of the market. That if something isn't done soon (i.e., government intervention), no one will be able to afford health insurance in the future.

But these supposedly evil corporations are not the ones to blame. So who is to blame? The people of this country that spend their money on big-screen TVs instead of health insurance. That may seem like a cold way to put things, but there are millions of Americans who could afford some form of health care if they budgeted carefully and worked toward securing a better job and a better future.

These people, many of whom are young and believe they won't need medical attention any time soon, end up in the emergency room or operating table. They have emergency procedures done, which hospitals are required to provide, and end up owing thousands and thousands of dollars to these institutions. Without insurance, they leave the hospital tens of thousands of dollars in debt and unable or unwilling to pay.

So now you have hospitals holding the bag for work that will cost them millions of dollars a year, if you add up all the uninsured they've treated. Where are they going to get this money do you think? They are going to get it from the insurance companies and from the government. The government can't afford to cover it all, and so hospitals pad the bills of those who do have insurance? A pair of crutches for your sprained ankle? That'll be $250 please. A night in the ICU? That'll be seven-thousand-plus dollars, thank you.

These services don't cost that much, but the hospital needs the money from wherever they can get it. And despite charging exorbitant fees to the insurance companies and their patients, most hospitals are still losing money hand over foot.

The insurance companies know about overcharging practices, and they also know that the only way they can afford to pay for them is to charge more for their own services. Those costs end up coming out of the pockets of employers and employees alike. And the more expensive they get, the fewer employers can offer them to their workers. More people go uninsured and more costs rack up.

This vicious cycle goes on and on, escalating the costs of medical care to heights that are not in line with the normal increases for costs of living and inflation. And it all starts with the people too irresponsible to insure themselves against an emergency.

The consequences of this health-care nightmare are devastating to the economy. Billions are spent every year by employers just trying to offer some semblance of benefits to their employees. They have less money for research and development, fewer dollars to hire new help, and even fewer profits to put back into the economy.

Health care is an anchor that is dragging down our economy, and now the government wants to wade in to "fix" the problem by offering a public health-care option. An option that could cost $1 trillion over the next ten years. And who's going to come up with that $1 trillion? That's right, the same beleaguered workers who are desperately trying to hold on to their own health insurance. The health insurance they are paying for out of their own pockets with the help of their employers.

Health care is a major drain because it is supporting people who were irresponsible growing up; people who didn't secure themselves coverage by working hard in school and by assuring themselves the skills necessary to find good jobs.

By doling out money to every American in need of health care, we make providing care a job not worth having. Doctors will earn less, and the wait for proper care will get longer as doctors start to care less about providing top-notch care.

Doctors are already under immense strain financially because of malpractice lawsuits, many of which are frivolous. Caring for Americans has become a job of restraint and limitations. Not only do physicians have to worry about who might sue them, they also have to worry about getting paid for the work they do accomplish. And now the government wants to add another layer of bureaucracy to that? How is that going to make things better?

Before the healthcare legislation passed, according to polls over 80% of people were happy with their healthcare. However, when healthcare is taken over by the government, there will definitely be rationing of care. A government bureaucrat will decide if your life is worth saving or not. There is no way around it, rationing of healthcare is required when the government has a healthcare budget and an ever increasing number of people enrolling in government controlled healthcare. So the government will provide a minimal level of services to those whom are deemed worthy of the investment. In other words, a 75 year old person who has paid taxes his entire life may be denied life saving surgery because it will be deemed too expensive. This is because the future tax revenue from that patient may be less than the cost of the operation.

Health-care Legislation

For most of 2009, President Obama tried his best to get a health-care bill passed. His party leaders in the Senate and House of Representatives, Senator Harry Reid and Congresswoman Nancy Pelosi, offered handouts on an unprecedented scale in return for votes. Billions were added to many versions of the bill as President Obama pushed for something, anything to be passed so that he didn't look as though he'd wasted a year chasing reform that never passed.

Well, guess what? In early 2010, the citizens of Massachusetts decided they'd had enough of the Democrats pushing legislation through the congress that didn't live up to anyone's standards. After the death of Senator Ted Kennedy, the citizens of Massachusetts elected, for the first time in decades, a Republican to represent them. They elected Senator Scott Brown because they believed that Democrats had to be stopped before they pushed through a bloated, ineffective health-care bill that did nothing to correct the fundamental problems in our health-care system.

You see, the Democrats had sixty senators before Brown's election. That meant they could pass any legislation they wanted because they could overrule any Republican filibuster. But with Brown's election, the Republicans had forty-one votes and could block legislation if they deemed it unfair. This doesn't mean that no compromises would be made, but it meant that legislation couldn't be forced on the Republicans.

Filibuster: the right of a senator to unlimited debate. This means that if a senator wants to block legislation, he or she can speak on the floor of the Senate indefinitely on any topic he or she chooses. This is designed to halt the process of passing legislation and can only be overturned by a vote of sixty senators, which the Democrats had at one point. So why would a senator want to do this? If one party is well short of the votes needed to stop legislation they deem as unfair, they use a filibuster as a last resort.

As a sign of how poisonous the health-care bill had become, the Democratic Party had to convince many of its own members to support the bill by essentially paying them off. Senator Ben Nelson of Nebraska, a Democrat, was given the sweetest deal of all. His state's Medicaid costs will be paid for by the federal government . . . forever. That's right, forever.

Senator Mary Landrieu of Louisiana asked for, and received, $300 million in Medicaid funding for her state just to begin *listening* to a debate on passing the bill. What she and the other senators like her did was disgusting. It was blind robbery of the American people, and it ought to be treated as such. She and her fellow senators should be treated the same way we treat other thieves: they should be thrown in jail.

What is so sad about this situation is that this is how the Senate and the House of Representatives do business on a daily basis. Senator Reid said, "That's what legislating is all about. It's compromise." I don't see much compromise in the way he got the bill to pass. He gave away the store in order to get it done and cost the country billions of dollars.

One important topic we need to discuss is the concept of insurance. Whether it is automobile or healthcare insurance, it should protect you from a catastrophic loss of money. You don't want to be stuck with a $25,000 bill from the hospital, but you shouldn't expect insurance to cover you for every time you see your doctor for a wart or a sore throat. Those expenses are not catastrophic and you shouldn't purchase insurance to pay for them. The difference between the fist dollars you pay towards your healthcare and the amount of money, which the insurance pays, is known as the deductable. The higher the deductable the less money you pay each month for insurance.

With the advent of HMOs people have gotten used to the advent of co-pay and the insurance will pay the rest. This has led to the mentality that people believe everything should be covered and their healthcare is only worth the $20 co-pay. If each person had to pay a little more before they would use the doctor less, as opposed to if healthcare was very cheap the patients will abuse it and visit the doctors frequently, putting an extensive burden on the government (tax payer) to pay for all of those visits. If there were very high deductibles, the people would do the rationing on when to see the doctor, knowing that they are covered for a catastrophic illness. It boils down to control. In a government system, they control who gets what treatments. On the other hand, in a private system with a high deductable, you decide which treatments you need to get and you ration your own healthcare.

Broken from the Bottom-up

Our economy, as made clear in the health-care mess, is broken from the bottom-up, not the top-down. It is not the wealthy squeezing the poor but, rather, the irresponsible squeezing the responsible. There is a class of Americans who have grown up without making any efforts to secure their futures. Their futures have now become the present, and now we're all paying for their irresponsibility.

Wealth holds a place of duality in the United States. The American dream is an economic one in that it's said you can pull yourself up by the bootstraps and become wealthy even if you were born poor. In many countries, where social castes are set in stone, a poor person has no chance of becoming wealthy because they are refused opportunities afforded to those born wealthy.

It's still hard to go from poor to rich in this country because the wealthy have advantages in schooling and business networking. But it is possible. And millions of Americans dream every day of doing exactly that.

Unfortunately, millions of Americans hold a disdain for the wealthy. Even if they are the same Americans that one day dream of *becoming* wealthy. We hate the rich, but we desperately want to be one of them.

This duplicity on the part of the nation is an excuse for politicians to attack the wealthy with little fear of retribution. As long as they show the majority of voters that they are taking it to the "man" in the form of wealthy business owners, they'll get support come election day. They can stay in office in perpetuity, and that makes them powerful.

But it's a lie because those same politicians make millions of dollars working for the "bad guys" as consultants and CEOs when they do finally decide to leave office. They too want to become wealthy; they too love money.

The result of this treachery is that the wealthy, the ones who employ the rest of us, are taxed at exorbitant rates, made the villains in any problem the country has, and pointed to when looking for answers to the economic collapse. Because obviously, anyone with money is getting away with something.

The reality is, though, that the wealthy pay a huge percentage of the income taxes paid in this country. While the top 1 percent of wealthy individuals in the United States pay 40.4 percent of all federal income taxes. That's 40 percent!!!

And before you assume that's because they earn 80 percent of all wealth, the IRS says otherwise. The wealthiest 1 percent of Americans account for 22.8 percent of adjusted gross income as recently as 2007.

So the wealthiest individuals account for almost half of all taxes paid to the federal government. That means there is a huge class of individuals *not* paying that much into the pot. In fact, according to the CBO (Congressional Budget Office), the lowest fifth of earners in this country pay just 4.3 percent in effective tax rates.

Currently, our nation follows a progressive tax structure. In this system, the more money you make, the higher percentage you pay in taxes. The government is redistributing the money and, in turn, punishing success.

Our nation should have a flat tax; regressive tax; or, maybe the best option of all, a consumption tax. We want to encourage people to make more money, not penalize them for making more money. If we had a flat tax, everyone pays the same percentage regardless of income. In a regressive tax, the tax rate incrementally goes down as income increases. With more money to reinvest in businesses and personal purchases, more money will flow into the economy.

In a consumption tax, people would not be taxed on the federal level on their income, instead only on their consumption. When people buy products, with the exception of food, you pay a high tax rate on these products. That way, people pay taxes on excessive luxury items and people will have more money in their pocket (because they aren't paying federal income tax) to buy these items.

In a flat-tax system, everybody pays the same percentage of his or her income regardless of how much that income is. Experts say that the government would not lose any tax revenue this way; contrarily, they would actually increase it.

In a regressive tax system, the percent of income taxed decreases the more money you make. For example, if people paid a tax rate of 10 percent on the first $50,000 instead of the rate going up as you make more money, the rate would actually decrease as you make money. For example, if you pay 10 percent on the first $50,000, you would pay, say, 8 percent on the next $50,000, and 6 percent on the $100,000 after that. A person making $50,000 pays $5,000 in taxes. A person making $150,000 pays the $5,000 plus $4,000 for his or her next $50,000 and $3,000 on their next $50,000 for a total of $12,000. So the government is making 2.5 times the amount of money from that person, yet he still has the incentive to make more money.

We're not including these statistics to say that wealthy people are saints or that poor people should be taxed at much higher rates. We're including these statistics to point out that the Americans' money problems *are not* the result of the wealthiest individuals in America even though many Americans believe these people don't pay taxes at all. Not only are they paying the taxes, but they are also creating jobs that allow other people to pay taxes. The wealthy people hire people to do services, they buy products, and they make the economic engine of this country possible. Why would you attack the people who are creating the jobs in this country while sparing those who don't create jobs? The reason is obvious: votes. So instead of creating a country that rewards hard work, you create a country that penalizes it. This is a recipe for failure and cannot be sustained.

Wealthy Americans are giving as much as a third of all of their income to the federal government every year. And they're giving up more to their state and local governments. They are providing billions of dollars to support those people who were irresponsible in their youths and are now on the perpetual welfare wheel.

And so what does President Obama propose we do to pay for his new health-care plan? He proposes we increase taxes on those families making more than $250,000 because they can afford to give more. He hasn't proposed taxes on those making less than that so far, though he has passed into law as part of his health-care bill a penalty on all families who don't buy health insurance. And maybe these families earning more than $250,000 can afford to give more, but that doesn't make it right. Our health-care system wouldn't need more money if those people who refused to get coverage were denied indefinite care.

Many of the hospitals in this country spend most of their time and money treating a small percentage of people who go to the emergency room again and again and again receiving drugs and treatment they will never ever pay for. These people are oftentimes drug addicts or the mentally disturbed, both of which need treatment and intervention.

The end result of all this is that you and me, and the wealthy are being squeezed by the government as they seek to prop up those of the unemployed and uninsured that are in their current life positions as a result of irresponsibility.

The fix for the economy is complex, and we'll discuss it more later in the book. But history has shown that cutting taxes on the business owners and wealth producers of the country produces greater economic growth than increased taxes ever will. It's called trickle-down economics: the hard workers keep more of their income and then subsequently spend more of it on products and services, which in turn secures jobs for more Americans.

Purple Pen versus Red Pen

So what should our government be doing with these companies and individuals that acted foolishly? What should our economy look like? Capitalism in its rawest form can be brutal to someone who jumps into it unprepared. It is a survival-of-the-fittest place that chews up the redundant among us and spits us out. Our country has never adopted this model. We have always had some form of regulation, and we should continue to do so in order to ensure best practices. But a return to the ideals of capitalism might just save us.

But we are afraid of failure in America, and it's going to be the end of us. Just look at how our schools are coddling students. Teachers now are made to mark kids' papers with purple pen instead of red pen because red pen has a "strong negative connotation." This is pathetic. Have we really gotten this insecure about failing? Imagine the economic fallout of letting all these banks fail, of letting all the individual families who borrowed too much get evicted from their homes. It would be awful. But the result would be a populace that learns the hard lessons and that is less likely to repeat their foibles.

Imagine if the thousands of workers at AIG who took part in ridiculous investment schemes were kicked to the curb and told to never come back. Imagine if Lehman Brothers wasn't the only Wall Street titan allowed to fail. These institutions would stand as lessons to us all, and our country would be better off because of it.

The message from the federal government would be "You mess up, it's on you." People would be a lot more careful with their money. Our economy, of course, would suffer for years as it recovered, but once people got the message that they had to stand up for themselves and their money, we could rebuild on the sound, conservative principles of wealth management that should be the bedrock of our economy.

Following the Great Depression, the generation that had lived through it as children were extremely careful with their money. They were the generation that wanted to put all their money under the mattress because they didn't trust banks. And they had good reason not to: banks had failed en masse because of panics and a lack of federal safety nets.

Safety nets, however, are different from ridiculous bailouts. Now we have reason not to trust banks because of federal intervention, not because of a lack of it. The generation that has lived through this recession should heed the advice of the generation that lived through the Great Depression: save your money for retirement, be conservative, and prepare for the worst.

Today's working generation is paying for an attitude that insisted on having all of it right now. Starter house? What's a starter house? I want a mansion. And I want the BMW to go with it. Aspiring for these things is fine if you can afford it and if you're willing to work for it. But many weren't, and they should have been allowed to fail miserably as they deserved to.

CHAPTER 4

OUR CULTURAL DIVIDES

"A house divided against itself cannot stand"
Abraham Lincoln, 1858

There are estimated to be at least eleven million illegal immigrants in the United States, but the true number is hard to know. After all, illegal immigrants don't exactly report themselves to the INS or the census bureau. While immigration, even illegal immigration, is not new to our country, the problems that we face today are complicated.

In recent years, activist groups have pushed for increased rights for illegals, arguing that those already within the borders should be allowed to stay under an amnesty plan that would grant them naturalized citizenship. Some say it could do no harm since they're already here and that our nation should be more accepting of immigrants of all stripes.

Our nation has traditionally been very accommodating when it came to immigration. In the early part of the twentieth century, a huge wave of immigrants came to this country from Europe and Asia. Millions of new Americans were brought through places like Ellis Island, and almost all were approved for immigration on the spot, barring disease. Getting to the United States was often a harrowing journey, but becoming an American was relatively easy.

Meritocracy

If you are a minority in this country, you will likely be treated as "different" many times in your life. Some of these moments will involve racism or negativity, and they might come from an unlikely source: affirmative action. You would think that programs designed to help minorities advance in the workplace would be a good thing considering the horrific history our country has had with African Americans in particular. But affirmative action only perpetuates stereotypes and furthers animosity between the races.

How is this possible? For years, African Americans fought to be treated as equals. Many died; and many more were injured, insulted, and marginalized by a society bent on keeping them in the shadows. It was our nation's darkest hour, and it lasted far too long. One of the movements that followed the civil rights movement was the push for affirmative action. It was thought at the time that by forcing largely white institutions to hire and promote more minorities, our nation could correct some of the transgressions of our past. It was a program started with good intentions. But like many things motivated by good intentions, it quickly turned bad.

Imagine how it feels to be a hardworking engineer or accountant or firefighter caught in the middle because of affirmative action. If you're good at your job and you earn a promotion, people will still look at you as having attained your position through affirmative action. A program designed to help people robs them of their dignity. Now imagine you aren't good at being an accountant or engineer. You still get a promotion because your company has to promote a certain number of minorities to comply with affirmative action. Now you've attained a position you aren't qualified for, and the people you work with are given a negative impression of affirmative action. Meanwhile, you've had your legs cut out from underneath you because no one respects your position.

There are definitely still companies in this country that overlook minorities because of racism. But the number of organizations that still do that is dwindling, and there are now more opportunities than ever before for people of all colors who work hard and become specialized in an in-demand field. You can achieve something without a special helping hand interfering, and the results of your work will be more rewarding.

The people advocating affirmative action are forgetting a few things. First, positions that are earned through mandate are not worth having. The lack of respect, the lack of authority, and the lack of that "I earned this" feeling can bring a person down. Second, affirmative action has done little to temper true racism. If people are judging someone by the color of their skin, they are going to do it regardless of the position they hold or what legislation is passed. And third, affirmative action has dictated that a certain group of people shall be advanced before others, regardless of the work done by those being promoted or those being passed over. This is a form of racism.

I have a dream that my four little children will one day live in a nation where they will not be judged by the color of their skin but by the content of their character.

—MLK Jr. in "I have a dream" speech

Martin Luther King Jr. was a great man. He understood that true equality means never judging someone based solely on their color, religion, or nationality. Imagine the message it sends to both parties when someone unqualified for a job is promoted to it based solely on a quota for how many people of a certain color must be advanced. Imagine the feelings from both parties.

Let's first imagine that you're the person being passed over for a job because your company has to promote minorities into certain positions. You've worked hard and set yourself up for the job. You believe you're qualified and you've put in the time and requisite effort to make yourself a strong candidate. Now the person that is promoted instead of you may very well be qualified. And if that is the case, you move on and try harder next time. But time has shown that when you mandate the hire or advancement of a certain number of any group, you ask for trouble. There are times in every company or organization when the only qualified candidate (or even the most qualified candidate) is not a minority. In these cases, there are bound to be hurt feelings and unqualified candidates put into new positions.

These advancements send the wrong message to both parties. It says to the white candidate that no matter how hard you work or how qualified you are, there will be times when you passed over for your race. Sound familiar? That's because it's what happened to African Americans for years. It wasn't fair then, and it's not fair now.

To the candidate promoted without merit, the message is entirely different, especially if our hypothetical candidate is young and cannot remember the days when minorities had to fight tooth and nail for respect. The message sent is that you don't have to work harder than the next man or woman fighting for a job; you just have to be picked to fulfill the needs of a quota. That's a horrible message to send to someone who is new to the career world. The impressions formed can ruin someone's drive to work and to succeed on their own. The same is true for a white candidate overlooked because of his or her race: without a level playing field, there is little incentive to work hard.

Unfortunately, affirmative action hasn't just had a negative impact on the career world. Affirmative action initiatives start affecting people as early as in college.

Universities have for years set aside slots in their incoming classes for students whose parents cannot afford to pay the tuition. This has allowed many qualified students the chance to acquire an education that would otherwise be too expensive for them. It's a wonderful initiative, and it has helped to raise the level of student our nation produces. But that isn't where these initiatives stop. Students that aren't qualified for some of these schools are getting in on the basis of their race.

Schools have lowered their entrance criteria in an effort to force the issue of diversity. Many universities allow nonwhite students entrance with lower SAT scores because this standardized test is supposedly biased and not as easy for nonwhites. This, even though the SAT tests high-school-level math and English skills, skills supposedly taught equally to all groups in our public-school system. Again, affirmative action denies qualified kids a place in their schools of choice. Instead they allow into these schools students who have not worked as hard at learning basic math and English skills. Kids who haven't worked hard enough to get the grades they need for the best schools. Kids who should by all rights be "paying" for their lack of effort with fewer options for higher education.

Again, this is not to say that programs which help needy kids are wrong. But there is a difference between the African American student that gets straight As and who scores well on the SAT but simply cannot afford tuition and the kids that don't work as hard but get a pass anyways. There should be a solid distinction between these groups.

The programs that help the truly needy reinforce what the parents of poor but ultimately successful children have been teaching for years, that the way out of poverty is through education and hard work. That is the beauty of America! People come here with often no more than the shirts on their backs, and in one generation, their children are college students. That is through hard work, not government subsidies, such as affirmative action.

So what's the solution? It's simple. College entrance forms should not have any reference to race at all. There should not be a single question which asks you about your racial heritage. The entrance applications should be standardized at all public schools and should focus on academic achievement only, with emphasis toward grade point averages, SAT scores, academic awards and accomplishments, and extracurricular activities. Getting into a good school should have nothing to do with your racial background. It's not fair to treat people negatively based on their race, and that holds true in instances where kids are told they don't have to play by the same rules. It's insulting. It's like telling someone, "Oh, you're short, so we're going to lower the basket for you when you play basketball."

A win is only rewarding when it is achieved on a level playing field. Minority students don't want to be treated any differently than anyone else. They don't want to be held back because of their race, and they don't want to be given advantages not given to their peers. Giving them unwanted perks or penalties taints the experience and emphasizes that they are "different" just as much a racial taunt might.

Our government really has only a couple of jobs when it comes to education: to make sure our schools are safe and hold everyone to the same standards. Our schools should be places where we promote education and learning, and those who choose to excel can do so. There should not be a "diploma factory" mentality among educators anxious to move people along. If a student chooses not to be engaged in the process, he or she should be held back until they decide to engage.

Assimilation

Now getting into the country, especially through Mexico, seems easy by comparison but becoming an American citizen can take years. So how are these new immigrants different from the ones that flooded the country a century ago? Assimilation. Or a lack of it.

Though our country has been called a "melting pot," a term you may have heard in your history classes, the reality is that we have long been divided by social, racial, and economic lines, more like a salad bowl. Our nation often demands conformity before acceptance and so new arrivals in the twentieth century were forced to assimilate (often for a couple of generations) before being accepted.

People from all over the world come to America because it is a melting pot. Because if you have a dream to succeed, you will be able to do so. America is the beacon of hope around the world because anyone can come here and have opportunities to prosper. But in order to succeed, you have to assimilate into the society, you cannot expect the society to assimilate to you. If we all work together as Americans, we accomplish great things.

Because of this attitude, most immigrants forced their children to learn English. In fact, many refused to allow their children to speak the language of their origin nation. It was a tough transition, but they realized the opportunity they had in becoming Americans and how important it was to leave behind old allegiances.

Today's immigrants are increasingly shunning the idea that English is necessary or that they should pledge allegiance to the United States before any other nation. And they're being aided in their refusal to assimilate by activist groups who are pushing for Spanish-language classes in American schools and who assert that illegal immigrants should be granted the same rights as American citizens.

The problem, of course, is that you can only truly be loyal to one nation at a time. You must make a choice and stick with it because loyalty cannot be done in half measures. Being loyal to two countries is like being loyal to two girls (or boys) at the same time; it can't really happen.

These divided loyalties—among millions of residents in our country—are tearing us apart. Our cohesiveness as a nation cannot survive if as many as twenty million people lean toward support of another nation.

A good example of this divided loyalty can be seen in the protests immigrant groups often stage when faced with a new round of proposed legislation calling for tougher sanctions against illegals. If you watch these protests, you'll see an amazing thing: a virtual United Nations' worth of flags being carried by protestors. Mexican, Panamanian, Honduran, and Nicaraguan flags being waved. Among these flags you often find American flags being waved as well. But which is it?

If illegal immigrants truly want to be American, why are so many holding fast to their nations of origin? Being proud of your heritage is admirable, but refusing to learn the language of your new nation and putting the flag of your native homeland above that of your chosen one is a recipe for disaster. It sends a signal that these immigrants want desperately to enjoy the rights of an American but want to do so on their own terms. America was made great because of immigrants. Immigrants who were willing to adopt the culture and values that make America great.

Imagine a classmate who kept asking to borrow your notes in order to study for upcoming tests but who refused to help you study when you needed help. It's the same concept, and it all begins with language.

So why doesn't the government want English to be the official language? The government thinks that by marginalizing immigrants it can keep them separate and make them stick together and vote as one block. And guess what party they will vote for? The party that will give them the most handouts. So the so-called nice party is actually preventing them from assimilating into the culture, preventing them from helping make America great, and keeping them down into subservient labor-intensive jobs. This is truly disgusting, but it is quite obvious.

Recent census data finds that 49% of all babies born in the United States are considered minorities. Lets see why this is important. Many of the minorities emigrated from countries with socialist or oppressive governments. These immigrants may not have a good understanding of the founding of the United States and our Constitution. Our constitution limits the power of the federal government.

The more citizens in the country that have no relationship with our founding and our Constitution the further away we get from the values and ideals of the constitution. It is like the telephone game, the more people playing the game, the further from the truth the last person is. So imagine after generations of immigrants the value of our Constitution will be totally lost. We will find ourselves living in a land with a powerful federal government that in no way resembles the country that became the beacon of hope across the world. It is incumbent upon everyone in society study the founding of our country and the Constitution that makes our country the greatest country on earth.

Muslims and Assimilation

This is a topic that most people are afraid to talk about for fear of being called bigoted. But the truth is that Muslims in many countries refuse to assimilate. They expect the countries they live in to adapt to their needs and lifestyles. That is true in Europe, and it is true in the United States. Many Muslims see themselves as loyal first to their religions and second to their countries. In fact, in a poll conducted by the Pew Research Center, Muslims around the world overwhelmingly identified themselves as Muslim first and a citizen of their countries second. For example, in Germany, 81 percent of Muslims lean toward religious identity first. And while Muslims tended to be more positive toward the current state of their nations than other citizens were, many people still distrust Muslims and fear that without a solid loyalty to their country, they are easily swayed to do things that are radical and dangerous.

What is so dangerous about the Muslims who refuse to be loyal to their countries is that they taint the reputation and level of trust of all Muslims. Many of our finest Americans are Muslim, but they are treated as radicals because so much of the Muslim populations give the impression that they are not interested in pledging allegiance to any entity other than their religion.

English as the Official Language

English is the key to success in our nation, even though many activists believe Spanish speakers should be accommodated even more than they already are. English means access to jobs that are better paying than the manual-labor jobs that so many illegal immigrants work when they arrive here.

Yes, these manual labor jobs pay better than many of the more advanced jobs these immigrants held back home do. Even engineers and doctors sometimes leave their home nations in order to work construction jobs here, knowing that the pay is ultimately better. But there are several problems with this.

First, our nation is being deprived of good pay for our own manual laborers. Not all the jobs being taken by illegal immigrants are undesirable. But most are, and by allowing these immigrants to avoid learning English, we keep them in these positions indefinitely.

Second, a common language creates a bond between the people of a nation. Without that bond and with continued allegiance to various foreign nations, the people of the United States are being divided along geographical lines. It's a situation that will only get worse if more and more immigrants—including those from Europe or Africa—come to this nation and refuse to learn English.

The primary divide in our country is obviously Spanish and English. Call any major company's customer assistance line and you have a choice of the two languages. Press 1 for English; press 2 for Spanish. What this divide has done is to create a shadow economy, one in which Spanish speakers are able to operate (work, shop, sell, trade) without ever taking part in the English-speaking United States.

We have always had neighborhoods where one language was spoken predominantly over English, places such as Little Italy, Little Havana, etc. But never before has a foreign language taken such a profound role in our society. Today, a Spanish speaker can go through their everyday lives without the benefit of English. They can keep up with the news on Spanish-language television networks or in Spanish newspapers. They can go to restaurants, jobs, and more, all in their native tongue.

English-speaking Americans can't always say the same. Many of the restaurants we go to, including McDonald's, are devoid of proficient English speakers. We struggle to find someone in the building who can answer a question more complex than "How much?" And the result is animosity and the creation of two worlds operating separately instead of in unison.

If the immigrant community wants to be better understood—and by all means they have a great deal to offer our country—they should make the commitment to learn English as their first priority. In fact, it ought to be required learning before citizenship is granted. With a language test attached to the citizenship exam, the government could force the hand of immigrants living in these parallel economies. The results would be beneficial to everyone:

- More participation in white-collar jobs by qualified, legal immigrants
- A reality closer to the "melting pot" depiction of our country
- A more realistic process for dealing with legal immigrants

Without an official language that everyone participates in using, our country will end up dividing into more and more segregated communities. Perhaps communities that don't interact with one another. We will be a nation divided.

The Bible provides us with a powerful story to demonstrate the power of language. The Tower of Babel was built by the people of Babylon, the survivors of the great flood, and their ancestors. These people spoke one language and were united in their efforts to build a tower that glorified their people.

As a punishment for their arrogance and their attempts to worship man over Himself, God broke up the peoples of Babylon by confusing their languages and by scattering them across the face of the earth. As you can imagine, not being able to understand their neighbors didn't engender goodwill among the peoples of the Earth.

This is not to say that warfare will break out or that immigrants should be forcibly made to learn English under some government program. But there ought to be come recognition that learning the language of your adopted country makes life easier for everyone. And it should be a mandate before citizenship can be granted that applicants speak English. This saves money for the schools and provides immigrants with opportunities for entering into better jobs and that it helps to bind the disparate cultures in our nation.

How You Can Help

If you're a student and reading this, you may wonder how you can help or even how this affects you. If you live in the Southwest, however, you have probably seen this issue play out in your own schools, or perhaps you are the child of an illegal immigrant. Whatever the case may be, there are several things you can do to help the situation.

First, be helpful to those people trying to learn English in your schools. There will be students who speak Spanish or another language and are genuinely trying to assimilate into our culture. Help them if you can.

Second, write to your representatives and let them know that you want tighter border security. Tell them how you feel about the issue and that you're worried about the future state of your government and your economy.

Third, work hard and make sure that as you invest in this economy, you hire Americans to do your work. That can be any American, whether naturalized or a recent immigrant who has come here legally looking for opportunity. The reason so many illegal immigrants skirt the law is that it is easy to find employment no matter where they go. Without this support, they will be forced to work through proper channels.

CHAPTER 5

THE AMERICAN WORKER

Becoming a part of the American workforce can be a blessing and curse. You are part of the most dynamic, rewarding economies in the world, and the possibilities are limitless. You can, if you work hard enough, excel at what you do and create a wonderful career that pays well. On the other hand, the incentives for following this path have been evaporating as government intervention in private business has spiked in recent years.

The reason the United States is known as the land of opportunity is that there is no set class system. If you can create a smart-enough business idea and follow through on its growth, then you too can become wealthy. It doesn't matter where you start in life in the United States; there has always been an opportunity to go from rags to riches. And while those opportunities still exist, you have to ask yourself what awaits you on the other side of your journey to success.

The business owners of today were the dreamers of yesterday. They had the guts and tenacity to build successful enterprises so that they too could have the satisfaction of building something great. But their reward has not been a pat on the back or smart regulation by a small efficient government. Their reward has been a government which now seeks to punish them with higher taxes, required health-care offerings for their employees, and bailouts for their competition, the same competition that couldn't cut it in the market.

As a matter of fact, the Obama administration is trying to marginalize the successful people. They are trying to make it seem like anyone who earns over 250K has so much extra money that they can spare some to spread the wealth around. In true communist (progressive) societies, the rich being villainized and having their money stolen from them by one tax after another. These are the people that are living the American dream and through hard work and dedication rose through whatever obstacles were in their way and were able to reach their goals. They played the game within the rules, and instead of being applauded and being seen as examples of what makes America great, this communist administration has relentlessly attacked them and made them out to look evil. This is a fundamental transformation from a country that cherishes success and rewards hard work to a country that forcibly redistributes the wealth for the false belief of creating social and economic justice. Make no mistake about it; the plan for fundamental transformation that President Obama so routinely speaks about is a plan that strays away from the principles of our founding fathers and heads toward the dark waters of socialism, Marxism, and communism.

There is little incentive now for someone to risk their own time and money in starting a business that will not ever have an advantage over a competition that is artificially propped up by the government. There will still be opportunity, but how can you be sure that you'll ever "win" over the competition in what is supposed to be a free market?

The way to fix a failing economy is creation of wealth, not redistribution of wealth. If the bottom or the foundation of a society is struggling, you do not pull the top. You reinforce the bottom. You can make English the official language. You can teach personal responsibility. You stop doling encouraging welfare as an acceptable lifestyle. Stop taking from the successful and start aspiring to be them. Stop looking for shortcuts or easy fixes and instead encourage hard work and dedication. Don't expect the government to be responsible for you. When you have a strong sense of work and a strong sense of family, you don't need the government as your baby daddy.

President Obama's answer to the failing economy was a ginormous government-spending bill using money that America doesn't have and that we will need to borrow. This money is used to create government jobs and grow the size of the government. If you really want to stimulate the economy, it is very simple: drastically reduce and limit taxes. Imagine if the single biggest financial burden that every single person faces (taxes) were removed. People would have up to 50 percent more money to spend, and they will spend it. They will hire workers, who will spend money. They will buy goods and services that spread money. The economy would turn around so fast the president Obama's head would spin.

Speaking of strong sense of family, this is an important time to mention that the traditional family unit of a mother and father living at home with their children offers the child the greatest chance of success. Of course there are exceptions to every rule, but societies with high teenage-pregnancy rate (the United States is number one of all developed countries in the world) or births to unwed mothers cannot compete with societies that value the traditional family. It is hard enough to successfully raise a child with a mother and father in the house. Imagine how difficult it is when you are the only parent who has to both work and raise your kids. The government can be easily assumed to be the baby daddy and to provide all the things that a family would normally provide such as health care, food, and education. The government gets its money from people like you, and you cannot afford to take care of everybody's baby. A lesson of responsibility needs to be taught, and there should not be families that are too big to be sustained.

The lack of incentive for business ownership is just one of the major problems with the situation American workers find themselves dealing with. There are problems with unions, problems with education, and problems with the attitude many Americans have developed toward working in general.

The Problem with Unions

Early in the twentieth century, working conditions in our nation were horrible for many, many workers. Legal immigrants and Americans alike were forced to work long hours with no benefits and no one looking out for their safety or their rights as workers. They didn't have rights. The solution for fighting back against corrupt businesses was to unite, to form unions for workers.

This process was difficult to say the least. Employers at the time, especially large employers, wanted nothing to do with unionized employees. They knew that having to pay higher wages for fewer hours worked would cost them dearly, and they retaliated swiftly and violently. They hired "union busters" to break up rallies through force and did all they could to prevent reforms.

The unions were ultimately successful (after many a bloody confrontation) in winning rights for workers. They helped with the creation of the forty-hour workweek and even the weekend (imagine not having a weekend). They ensured that companies offered health benefits and were instrumental in the creation of pensions. Unions were a necessary countermeasure to the business practices of so many companies then.

At one time, millions and millions of Americans were part of unions, and to say you were a union-man meant that you would stand up for your coworkers against unfair business practices. But things have changed in the United States. Workers for the most part are no longer subjected to physical abuse or threats of violence from their employers. Conflicts now relate to the increasing rarity of health benefits and the lack of security in today's economy. So what are the unions to do?

You see, unions are like any other business entity: they need to sustain themselves, even if their original mission is no longer needed as much as it once was. Union leaders are now just as concerned with keeping their own jobs (some of which pay very, very well) than they are with protecting their members.

Here's an example: the three-strikes-you're-out legislation that puts repeat felony offenders away for life after they commit their third felony. Some would say this legislation is the result of legislators who want to be tough on crime, or one the public's desire for safer streets and fewer career criminals on the loose. The reality? The legislation, which had its origins in California, was greatly influenced by the California Correctional Peace Officers Association.

You may be wondering why corrections officers would be influencing legislation on matters outside of the prison system. Yes, they are affected by criminal activity of all kinds, but what about this particular legislation was so important? Jobs. That's right: jobs for their members.

According to a report first aired on NPR in August of 2009, the CCPOA played a crucial role in the passing of referendums that were designed to get tough on crime. The voters of California were blitzed with TV ads, pamphlets, and other advertisements created by Governor Pete Wilson. It worked. The voters supported these referendums, and the prison population skyrocketed from 20,000 inmates to 167,000. Shortly after he backed the new laws, the union donated $1 million to Governor Wilson.

As a result of the new laws, and the ever-growing prison population, the union's workers were now in more demand than ever. New prisons were built and more guards hired, and the union grew more powerful. But the results were not good for the voters who had supported the legislation. Once a model for other prison systems, California's fell apart under increased costs and overcrowding. The recidivism rate went up, and prison violence exploded. Now the Californian government is bankrupt, and so they are trying to release 6,500 inmates into the streets to save money.

The union had one thing in mind: increase our political presence and fatten our coffers. Unfortunately, this attitude is prevalent among modern-day unions, even as their numbers have dwindled. Though they now represent just 7 percent of American workers, unions are bowed to the Democrats. Democratic presidents have always drawn on the support of unions which essentially tell their members which way to vote. Instead of having to win over millions of individual voters, the Democrats had merely to win over the union leadership and they were assured of thousands and thousands of supporters.

This relationship can lead to only one thing: corruption. Corruption has always been a part of unions, mainly because unions controlled millions of dollars in pension money and because a handful of people are in charge of millions of voters, voters that can swing the outcomes of some very important elections. Being in a position that holds so much power is bound to tempt anyone, but time and time again it has been shown that today's union leaders are susceptible to being bribed.

Unions are good for guaranteeing wages but can also stand in the way of the progress of a company. You're either on the team or not when it comes to business, and many union members are on the "union" team and not that of the company. The number one thing in business should be allegiance to the company. As an example of the skewed power base that unions have built for themselves, look at the bankruptcy of Chrysler. The bondholders in the company (the people who had invested their own money in the company's stock) were given just two percent of the company during the bankruptcy. The union members were given 10 percent.

Our Schools Need Help

Our new employment landscape is unsuitable for the lazy or self-important. Finding a job now means becoming more specialized than the next person in line, and becoming more specialized means more schooling. Schooling takes discipline and effort. So you would think the cream would rise to the top.

Unfortunately, American schools don't foster competitive, hardworking kids, rewarding them with recognition and increased support. Instead, our schools seek to squash the differences between children, to stamp out any idea that one child is smarter or harder working than the others. We're all the same, after all, and everyone is special.

Americans have traditionally been known as hard workers. In fact, Americans are sometimes considered obsessed with work; the population averages more work hours per week than almost any other nation on earth. Of course, because of our problem with obesity, we're also called lazy. So which is it?

It's both. America is in the midst of a transition when it comes to how we work. Our spending power has not improved in many years; and so we have more couples working, more hours worked, and more people with multiple jobs than we've ever had. But does that mean the work ethic that made this country into an economic powerhouse is still alive and kicking? No.

There are, of course, millions of hardworking Americans, but our success has bred a new worker that feels entitled to a management job straight out of college and—prior to the economic collapse—a belief that all jobs were temporary. This attitude meant that managers couldn't openly discipline or criticize their young workers because these workers would simply quit assured of another job in a booming economy. With an attitude like that, it was no wonder the younger generations in the 1990s and 2000s were called the "do nothing" generation.

So where did this attitude come from? Some of it came from the incredible growth of our economy. For years, a high-school graduate could be assured that if they worked hard, they could find a manufacturing or skilled-labor job at a company they would be part of until retirement. Their pay was enough to buy a home and support a family, and they would have good benefits (in part because of unions). But those jobs are gradually becoming rare in the United States.

Our manufacturing jobs have gone overseas to places where labor is cheap. Finding a job now requires more schooling and more hard work. But our success has made us comfortable. The generation whose children are now entering the workforce made sure that their children were well taken care of. These new workers never had to fight for anything or to endure a job market that was quickly losing jobs.

Figuring out what you want to do in life isn't easy. There are a lot of decisions to make and, hopefully, options to choose from in higher education. If you're privileged enough to be able to attend college, you've probably realized that not all the people going with you have put a great deal of effort into getting there. But even those kids that aren't giving their all are probably going to get a degree.

So much of our national identity is centered on the individual: the rights of the individual, the expression of the individual, and the accomplishment of the individual. But that focus has had consequences: parents have tried desperately to shelter their children from failure, to make them feel that as individuals they too are special. And our schools have gone along with this thinking. The result has been students who showed little effort in school flooding the marketplace.

Unfortunately, these same students are the ones who grow up to buy homes they can't afford and to pay for, the same ones being supported by bailout programs and increased unemployment and welfare. These students may become ill prepared to succeed and find it difficult to hold a steady job. In a sense, they are failing out of the postschool part of their lives because they were not pushed to their maximum capabilities while they were in school. Some may feel disenfranchised with the system and turn to the government to help them out.

The Lost Workday

According to a study performed by Salary.com and America Online in 2006, employee time-wasting costs American employers $544 billion a year! More than half of those surveyed for the study admitted that surfing the Internet was their primary distraction. The study showed that the average worker wastes about two hours of every workday, not including lunch and scheduled breaks.

If you factor in those breaks, which can sometimes add up to an additional hour or more, you have three hours of each eight-hour workday being lost to distraction. That's just over thirty-eight percent of each workday gone. Imagine the amount of work Americans could perform if they simply worked for the eight hours they were paid for.

In the recent economic downturn, it was found that even with fewer employees, most business felt no shortage of productivity. That's because each individual worker was afraid of losing his or her job and so had buckled down and started working as hard as he or she should have been working in the first place. In the same eight-hour day, these workers were producing much more work than they had previously, which I'm sure made their employers curious about what the problem was prior to layoffs.

Every employer knows that employees socializing, spacing out, or surfing the Internet will cost them time and money. Workers are not robots, and most people simply cannot concentrate and work for eight hours straight, day in and day out. The real problem isn't a lack of concentration though; it's a lack of consequences.

Employers are afraid to fire people nowadays, even people who are performing at incredibly low levels. Why? Because they are afraid of lawsuits. Every employer fears the disgruntled employees who sue the company for "wrongful termination" even if they were the laziest workers in the world. No one wants to take responsibility for their own actions, and if they get fired, it can't be because they weren't doing their work. It has to because someone is out to get them; someone is racist or sexist or has a grudge against them.

Companies in America today take great pains to make sure that if they fire someone they have documented very carefully the reasons why. Workers are now usually given two or three warnings (some of them verbal, some of them written) before they are fired. And that's the case even for workers whose behavior is horrible. This warning process, and the fear of litigation that created it, has led to workers feeling safe from being terminated. Workers know that before they get fired, they will receive warnings and they can simply work harder after each warning in order to save their jobs.

Let's face facts: most people will only do the minimum amount of work in order to keep their jobs. Most people don't have the self-discipline to make themselves work a solid eight hours each day, and the reality of the matter is they don't have to have it. They can coast through on the backs of those workers who really do produce a lot of work without fear of being fired.

There is a philosophy of human behavior in the workplace which states that 20 percent of the employees will cause 80 percent of the problems in a workplace and that 20 percent of the employees will produce 80 percent of the work. This principle is based partly on the work done by Dr. Joseph Juran, a quality-management pioneer, who did his most notable work in the 1940s and 1950s.

If you've ever worked in groups in school, you'll understand what this principle states. You've probably been a part of project groups that were supposed to divide the work equally among the members. But what happened instead? A small number of the students involved showed the initiative and produced nearly all the work. And what were the consequences for those students who didn't contribute anything to the project? Probably nothing. If your group received an A, then all the team members got an A.

Most students won't tell on their classmates for slacking off on a project, just as most employees won't tell on their coworkers for slacking off. So the cycle of laziness and lost productivity goes on and on. It's become so common for most of the workforce in a company to simply drag by, that it's almost accepted now. That has to change.

The standards we enforce in our schools and in our companies need a major overhaul. Our culture has come to accept that personal responsibility is someone else's problem. That kind of thinking would never fly in other cultures, especially in parts of Asia where a worker would be horribly embarrassed to be slacking off and not contributing to the whole effort of the company. Where is our shame? Why aren't we ashamed of being slackers?

In order to overcome our culture of shamelessness, teachers need to be tasked with enforcing higher standards for work in our schools. Slack off on a project? Get an F. Don't do your homework? Get an F. We cannot allow students to simply skate by without ever having to face negative feedback from an educator. We can't simply say "Oh, he's distracted" and then call it a day. Why? Because failing is important.

Failing teaches life lessons that cannot be replaced by a stern warning or by coddling. When you fail, you realize that success is not guaranteed, that in order to succeed you must change your attitude and your behavior. Failing also means that there are standards for success and that only those who put in the effort have a chance at advancing. Failing is necessary for building character and the drive to succeed. If we don't allow our kids to fail (or our country for that matter), we are doomed. Our country must be allowed to stumble, just as it did during the Great Depression. We come out of these periods stronger than ever.

A student who doesn't do his or work ought to be made to feel ashamed. Kids now can pass through high school with straight Es. The only way to actually not get credit for a class is to skip class too much. The student should be singled out and be forced to feel the humiliation of not pulling his or her weight. If you attend a modern American high school, you've probably seen students who simply do nothing. They sit around and crack jokes or text their friends, and when they fail to do their homework, they don't receive credit from the teacher.

I'm sorry to say this, especially if you're a student, but our kids are being coddled in a way that is setting them up to be a part of the 80 percent that contributes little to the overall productivity of the American workplace. These 80 percent were dubbed the "trivial many" by Dr. Juran, and his label is apt. When something is trivial, it doesn't matter. In many companies, a huge part of the workforce could be eliminated without a significant drop in productivity, as proven by the layoffs we've seen in this recession. That's a sad fact, but it's true.

If you've ever had a part-time or even full-time job, you've probably heard your coworkers moaning about the workload or how they're overwhelmed. This kind of ungrateful attitude has been tamped down somewhat by the recession because people are glad to have work, but it's another facet of laziness that goes unpunished in early education. When one employee, or student, constantly complains, the result is like a cancer: other workers start thinking it's okay to do the same, and this negativity spreads throughout the classroom or the organization. The 20 percent that causes 80 percent of the problems can be blamed for this as well.

Again, the government provides a safety net here where there should be none. Workers who are fired for lack of productivity are still able to get unemployment benefits in many cases because the *employer* has to prove the worker was fired for something that makes him or her ineligible for benefits. So even if a company manages to fire someone without getting sued, it still costs them money because they pay into an unemployment "bank" in many states to help cover the cost of unemployed workers. So the lazy, careless worker who gets fired is being treated by the government in the same way as someone who worked hard but was laid off because of a major loss in business for his company.

Workers who are fired "for cause," meaning they did something to get themselves canned, should not receive benefits of any kind. If you screw up, you should be fired and you should deal with the fallout from your decision to slack off. Your fellow employees have to pick up your workload, and it isn't fair to them that you are treated the same as they are when you lose your job.

Changing this horrid system will require a series of brave steps on the part of students, teachers, parents, and employers. Parents will need to understand that their kids are being punished because they did something wrong, and students will have to turn on their classmates when they don't hold up their end of the assignment. Teachers will need to be vigilant in enforcing homework and project deadlines, and employers will need to create an atmosphere where hard work is *expected*. As it stands today, many students and employees are treated to rewards simply for working hard. Working hard should be a minimum requirement for working at a job; it shouldn't be something that is unusual.

The Way out

You may not be a highly competitive student. You may not like school; not many people do. It can be boring and slow, and it can feel as though everyone is just passing through without any distinction between those who give their all and those who simply show up.

So what's the fix? How can we as a people change the way we support and reward hard workers? How can we make the workplace more competitive and more like our global competition?

It all starts at home and in the schools. The No Child Left Behind legislation has resulted in teachers teaching to a test. They must get all their students to pass the test with a certain score or they are punished. So what is the result? They have to focus their energies on the children they believe need the most help in passing the test. And what happens to the children who will pass easily, who are ready to advance to more difficult material? They are the ones left behind.

Schools should first be about helping students become competitive in a global economy. Hardworking achievement-driven students should be catered to and allowed to advance beyond their peers. Students who have genuine learning disabilities should be given the extra attention they need to learn, and the kids who put in little effort should be failed and forced to repeat the grade.

Our educational system, driven by advocates for more "progressive" education, has allowed students to simply float along with no real repercussions for failure. Schoolteachers are spending all their time disciplining students that should have been disciplined by their parents.

At home, parents need to be active in finding ways for their children to get engaged in early work programs. Internships and work-study programs are a great way to prepare future workers for the competitive world they'll be operating in. While parents can't necessarily change the school's policies, they can certainly push for classes that are smaller, for curriculum that doesn't teach down to the lowest denominator, and for classes that teach real life skills.

Another step parents can take is to support teachers in disciplining their children. Forty years ago, if a child went home to their parents and said they had been punished unfairly (most kids think all punishment is unfair), the parents would ask, "What did you do to get punished?" Parents today automatically assume their child is perfect and would therefore never need to be punished. Teachers are often confronted by parents questioning their motives and demanding a retraction of any punishment. This undermines a teacher's ability to effectively control his or her classroom and is another example of how personal responsibility is being assaulted in our country.

College Isn't the Only Way

Not everyone is destined, or even interested, in college. And that doesn't mean they aren't smart or capable people. Some kids are just looking for a profession that isn't emphasized by today's secondary school system. Traditionally, these kids would have looked to the skilled crafts—carpentry, auto repair, welding, etc.

So why are there now such a shortage of skilled craftsman in our country? If you look at some professions, for example, welding, there is a shortage of nearly two hundred thousand skilled workers, according to the American Welding Society. Welding is something that can provide job security. It can pay well, and if it is part of a repair or building construction, it can't be outsourced. So why haven't more kids taken up welding?

The answer is likely twofold. First, many American kids are told that skilled-labor jobs are only done by those people who *can't* go to college. The kids whose parents couldn't afford tuition and books or who didn't emphasize higher education. This attitude makes these professions seem less desirable as though working with your hands is something you do as a last result. It also fosters an attitude that people who work with their hands are automatically less intelligent than those people who have a liberal arts degree.

Second, there aren't that many opportunities for students who are interested in these professions to find quality training. They have to either apprentice to an established electrician or carpenter or welder or go to one of the few accredited trade schools around the country. These schools are often expensive and spread far around the nation, meaning many of their students have to move hundreds of miles to attend classes.

If we as a nation want to be "innovative" in the way we educate our students, we ought to rid ourselves of the idea that every students will do well in college if they are simply given the chance to attend. The increased focus on college has actually lowered the bar for education in our country because universities are admitting more students and lowering the standards for graduation.

When did we as a people start believing that manual labor of any kind was for "poor, uneducated" Americans who weren't smart enough to find a "good" job? The term *blue-collar* used to be a positive label given to someone who got up every day and went to work at one of the many factories or manufacturing plants in our country. It was a label of respect for the hardworking middle class in our country. However, with the loss of those jobs and the influx of cheap labor from the south, manual labor work has come to be associated with immigrants or with the uneducated who couldn't transition to information-based work.

We have lost people who know how to build things, who know what it means to deal with physical equipment. We have lost many of our nation's craftsmen to retirement, and they aren't being replaced. Many employers have complained about a lack of skilled workers applying for their available jobs, even during the recession. And that goes for jobs that aren't manual labor as well. Our students are simply not getting the skills they need to compete in the job market.

If you're a student looking at your options, keep in mind that there is good work for people with the right skills. Welding, carpentry, electrical work, auto repair, and other jobs are not lesser positions for people who can't afford college. They are positions that provide steady work and good pay. They are practical jobs that contribute real work to the economy, and there is nothing wrong with spending your career helping to build and repair our nation's infrastructure.

Many of the jobs in the new economy will be related to "green" technologies (we discuss this more in the chapter on the green revolution), and technicians will be needed to build the products. We have to use caution though in how we build up our green jobs. New technicians will also be needed to install things like solar panels and wind farms, but we want to make sure we don't shut out the workers in older technologies without giving them an option for finding good jobs. In Spain, for example, jobs are being lost as "green" jobs are added.

CHAPTER 6

BORDER SECURITY AND TOUGHER LEGISLATION

There has been a tremendous amount of debate in this country over what to do about illegal aliens. Some estimates put the number of illegal aliens in this country at more than twenty million. But to focus solely on illegal immigration is to miss the larger picture: securing the borders is the key to securing the nation as a whole.

Illegal aliens are not the only ones exploiting lax border security. There are literally millions of dollars worth of illegal drugs crossing the border from Mexico every day. Terrorists have been apprehended trying to enter the country illegally which we can assume means many more have gotten through. There are professional smugglers in Mexico that are hired to sneak Mexicans, terrorists, drugs, and weapons across the border into the United States. Young girls are being trafficked into the country to be used as sex slaves. These are just some of the problems our incompetent border security is allowing to happen. A sovereign nation must have control of its borders or it will fail to exist.

So what do you need to know about the problem that you aren't being told in school or on television? Well, first of all, the problems of border security aren't just ones of physical security. They are when it comes to terrorists and other criminals crossing, but the financial fallout can often be just as bad.

Before we get to those problems though, let's look at why immigration reform hasn't happened in any real way. If illegal immigrants are allowed into the country by an overwhelmed border patrol, they become a part of the national population. Democrats are in favor of an amnesty program which would allow many of these illegals to become citizens. If that happens, they will almost certainly all vote for the Democrats. It's a huge win for the Democrats because there could be as many as twenty million voters coming into their fold.

Take health care, for example. The health-care bill passed recently by the House and Senate will likely cost our country more than a trillion dollars. Most of the debate on the bill centered on the exorbitant costs for families, hospitals, insurers, and governments in trying to care for the sick. But the "solutions" in the bill center on the insurers and hospitals and employers in the middle of the entire process. No one is looking at illegal immigration or border security as being part of the health-care problem. Instead, Obama is focusing on trying to make sure illegals have access to health care.

Emergency rooms around the country are legally required to stabilize any patient that's brought to them. That doesn't mean they have to provide long-term care, but they do have to perform life-saving measures. Each of these incidences costs thousands of dollars. The illegal immigrants being brought in have no insurance and are unable to pay. The state and federal governments provide some support, but in the end the hospital doesn't make back its money.

And the problem really starts much sooner than the emergency rooms. The employers who hire illegal immigrants are not going to grant them any benefits. In fact, they aren't even likely to declare them as employees on their taxes. So not only does the government miss out on those pay roll taxes, but the illegals working with no benefits are unable to regularly see a doctor.

The result, of course, is that these undocumented workers are letting ailments go until they require emergency treatment. They fear being reported, and so even if they can afford it, many avoid going to a general practitioner. They have no photo ID and no insurance card, and so most doctors won't even see them. Many end up in hospitals for things that could have been addressed much sooner and with simple, relatively inexpensive medications.

Border Security

Why is border security so important? Why is it something that should concern the youth of this country? It seems as though most of the illegal immigrants coming into the country are simply looking for better pay than they can find in their native countries. Our country was made great by people coming here looking for a better life, so shouldn't we take the same attitude toward the people streaming over our borders every day? Not if they do it illegally. They should be using the front door to our country, not the back.

While it's true that most illegal immigrants are simply looking for better pay, the problem of border security has to do with much more than immigration. It spans a great number of things, not least of which is a multibillion-dollar drug industry that's flooding our streets with heroin, crystal methamphetamine, and cocaine/crack; cross-border crimes committed by these cartels including bribery of American officials; human trafficking; a lack of national security; and more.

We'll look at each one of these issues in more depth during this chapter, but let's start with just the idea of our borders being unsecured. Think about what that means in the bigger picture. A nation whose borders aren't secured can't really claim to be in control of overall security. Following 9/11, there were fears that terrorists could easily cross into the country through our porous borders. And unfortunately, the level of security we have at our borders hasn't improved. In fact, with the influx of drug money, the situation has become worse as more officials turn a blind eye to criminal activity.

Add on top of that the instability of Mexico, whose government has been under constant attack by drug cartels, and you have a major problem. While the illegal immigrants are costing us time, money, and manpower (in addition to jobs and tax income), it is the criminals we need to worry about most. The fact that they can so easily infiltrate our nation is frightening.

Imagine if your home had no locks. Now imagine that you had an open safe with millions of dollars in cash in it sitting in plain view of the windows in your home for all to see. How secure would you feel going to bed at night? Probably not very secure at all. Well, our nation is no different from that home when it comes to the drug cartels and terrorists.

Illegal immigration is a huge drain on our public resources. Not only do illegal immigrants not pay taxes, they use public funds for emergency medical care, the education of their children, and for many other public services. Public services should not be offered to people who are not citizens of the country.

Our country is one of the most lenient when it comes to people crossing out borders illegally. We are lenient for many reasons, one of which being that our country is one of the most attractive in the world for people seeking a better life. Compared to some nations, our treatment of illegal aliens could be considered plush.

When an illegal alien is caught within the United States, the punishment is usually nonexistent. We don't bother deporting most illegals, and in fact, if local authorities caught an illegal alien and called the feds, they'd be told not to bother. The feds are only worried about big numbers, and a single person isn't worth dealing with. If illegal aliens have committed a petty crime, they will likely be deported to their home countries, which they can then leave in order to illegally reenter the United States.

Some will say that we should be like other countries when it comes to handling illegal border crossings. For example, in nations such as China, Iran, or North Korea, illegal border crossings are treated as invasions of sorts, and the offenders are thrown in prison or worse. There is little leeway for forgiveness within these legal systems, and some would advocate a similar fate for those that cross our borders illegally. Obviously, violence is not the answer, but these countries put into stark contrast the way in which we treat people who have breached our border security.

First and foremost, let's look at what illegal immigrants do get if they should successfully breach our borders. Most, if not all, come here for work, and work they get. The economic slowdown has affected how many are getting work, but millions of illegal aliens have come here over the years and have been hired on the basis of no more than their job skills. Few are put through any kind of background check to see if they have a criminal past. Few are ever asked for proof of citizenship, and the ones that are can obtain fake social security cards and driver's licenses with just a few dollars and the right connections.

With this false identification, they can gain access to billions of dollars in social programs meant for struggling Americans. These social programs can include welfare, food stamps, or even subsidies to help pay for housing and job training. And in some instances they can vote. And their children can attend American schools, be treated at American hospitals, and essentially become Americans even though their parents gained access to the country illegally.

We treat illegal immigrants better than any nation on earth does, and so it makes sense that they keep coming into our country looking for work and the benefits of being de facto American citizens. And that trend won't stop until we reform what it is we offer to illegal immigrants and their children. As it stands now, the Fourteenth Amendment deems that you are an American citizen if you meet the following criterion: that you are born or naturalized in the United States. So if you go through the naturalization process (green card, etc.), you are a citizen. If you are born within the borders of our nation—including territories, etc.—you are a citizen. That means that if you're a foreign national looking to make a better life for your children, you'd do well to get across the border before they're born.

If you can get across the border and pay the money for the delivery within these borders (or just choose not to reimburse the hospital), you'll have a child that can grow up and enjoy all that this country has to offer. That's a lot of incentive to get into the country.

Just Saying No Isn't Enough

Our nation seems to have an insatiable appetite for illegal drugs. We are the largest purchasers of illegal drugs in the world because we have disposable income and the time to waste doing drugs. Our nation is rife with drug addicts and drug dealers. And so it's natural that the makers of these drugs will do whatever they can to bring the drugs into the country.

Unfortunately, any market that is this lucrative is bound to draw a great number of criminals into the fold. And these criminal cartels don't want to share the profits. They are also very well armed, and so naturally, violence becomes a part of the equation. Some would say that the violence is mostly Mexico's problem because it is the Mexican cartels fighting it out in the border towns. But they aren't limiting their fight to national borders, and we as Americans should be very concerned.

Americans have been kidnapped, murdered, and tortured by raiding parties that cross over the Mexican American border to capture them. They can easily make their way over into out towns to exact retribution on their perceived enemies or to monitor their drug stashes as they do in the Pacific Northwest, where teams of drug growers have taken over parts of our national forests.

If our borders aren't secured soon, the problems will only grow worse.

Human Trafficking

Every year, children your age and younger are brought into the United States for the purposes of slave labor and forced prostitution. These young people want nothing more than to find a better life in our country; but instead of applying legally, which can take years, they take a chance on the "coyotes" or people traffickers. These men and women are some of the lowest of the low, and they charge these young girls thousands of dollars each for passage into the country.

The problem, of course, is that these girls don't have thousands of dollars. In exchange for passage, they agree to work off the money they owe, essentially indentured servitude. But where is a young girl who may or may not speak English and who has no legal documentation going to get that kind of money? The answers are horrific.

These women are either made to do manual-labor jobs for virtually no pay or forced into prostitution. Of course, the people who force them into this life, the coyotes, have no interest in seeing them pay off their debts; so the girls are stuck in their miserable existence forever. It's a horrible way for a young person to spend their youth, and it's happening all too often.

The coyotes care little for their cargo should something go wrong, and it's not uncommon to hear of illegal immigrants who have died during passage into this country.

Terrorists Welcome

The attacks of 9/11 made everyone in the United States acutely aware of how real terrorism is. To many Americans, the 1995 bombing of the Murrah Federal Building in Oklahoma City was the act of a madman, not a terrorist. Even the 1993 bombing of the parking garage in the WTC wasn't enough to hammer home how immediate the threat is. But 9/11 woke everyone up. Too bad it was applauded by a good friend of our president's, Bill Ayers, Obama's longtime friend and radical communist, an unremorseful domestic terrorist who tried to bomb the Pentagon.

The fact is that our process of evaluating, monitoring, and controlling immigration is flawed and needs fixing. Foreign students are overstaying their student visas. Temporary workers are ignoring their established dates to return home. We know that terrorist cells are being developed in our country, and if we can't figure out who is coming and who is going, we're in some trouble.

Policing the Illegals

When illegal immigrants are pursued for breaking the law (which by entering the country illegally they are doing every day), they are pursued by law enforcement agencies. Some are local, some are state, and some are federal. These police officers and federal agents are risking their lives to pursue these immigrants. They are also being paid out of taxpayer dollars to do so.

The cost to communities across America is tremendous. Not only do the police departments have to stretch their budgets to pursue criminals who return to the country time and time again, but the psychological and practical toll on their communities also goes even deeper than money does. Communities are facing challenges like they've never seen before.

Most local police officers are not allowed to approach someone on the street and ask for proof of citizenship. Our Constitution protects us from illegal search and seizure, and so police officers must have probable cause to arrest or detain anyone, even if they suspect they are not citizens of this country and therefore not protected by the Constitution. It's a Catch-22 that is handcuffing many local police agencies and allowing the criminal faction of the illegal population to live and work here with the same rights as you or me.

In recent years, federal agencies have taken an approach that is slightly different in their attempts to find illegal immigrants working here in the United States. They have begun raiding businesses across the country and arresting and deporting many of the illegal immigrants employed here. They are also punishing businesses that offer employment to the illegals. But that's just a drop in the bucket as far the annual expenditures go.

Imagine you're a police officer and you are called to the scene of an accident. A speeding drunk driver has just plowed into a family of four, injuring everyone in the car. The drunk driver is unharmed, and as you approach his car, you prepare to arrest him for his actions. You get to the station and ask for identification. He has none. You ask for proof of auto insurance, required in every state. He has none. You ask for place of residence, but he has no official address because he's living illegally with twenty other immigrants in a one-family home. You call the federal authorities, but they don't want to deal with just one alien; they have far too many to deal with to get excited about that. So you detain the drunk driver and go through the expense of a trial for someone who can't afford an attorney. And then the jail has to use state money to house this individual.

But that's just the beginning. You see, that family of four had $250,000 in medical bills, which were paid partially by their own insurance company. But they are out of work for three months and their bills are piling up and they can't pay the hospital. But they have no legal recourse because how are they going to sue an illegal immigrant that has no property or insurance or even a driver's license?

This, of course, is a worst-case scenario, and it's not like the entire illegal population is out there wrecking cars. But this situation does, and has, happen. And the cost to communities and police departments and hospitals is tremendous. But President Obama refuses to really crack down on illegals because he'd rather see the country torn apart than miss out on critical votes.

Remittances

What are remittances? They are payments sent overseas by both legal and illegal immigrants. These payments go back to their families to help support them, usually in dire situations of poverty. So what does this have to do with you and me? A lot, as in billions and billions of dollars. That's right. Illegal immigrants are sending billions of dollars into foreign countries.

Illegal immigrants don't pay taxes. You wouldn't file a W-2 either if you were illegal. Why give the authorities a paper trail? That's billions of dollars not going to help pay for federal services. Services, by the way, that are often enjoyed by illegal immigrants. But wait, it gets worse.

The billions of dollars that are being sent overseas are not going back into our economy. Yes, illegals buy food and clothing, but they aren't spending their money on discretionary purchases. The economy in the United States is powered by the consumer. We buy things. We buy televisions and cars and houses and jewelry and shoes and everything else you can think of. Now imagine what kind of shape our economy would be in if the millions and millions of illegal immigrants paid taxes and kept their money here.

But we can't have it both ways. We can't lust after their taxes and disposable income and also want them to leave. But illegal immigrants can't enjoy the protections of our government and support of our civil infrastructure if they aren't going to pay taxes. They can't have their cake and eat it too any more than we can. If you want to be a part of the United States, you have to put down your stakes here, pay your taxes, and keep your money in the country.

PART II

THE FUTURE AND THE HOPE
FOR A BETTER AMERICA

CHAPTER 7

YOUR RESPONSIBILITIES
AS AN AMERICAN

"It's a free country." How often do you hear people say that when they don't agree with what you're doing or when they want to emphasize that their own behavior is okay because they have the right to act how they please? It usually goes something like this: "You want to throw your life away, be my guest. It's a free country." And yes, the United States is a free country in that its citizens are guaranteed certain rights. But as the old saying goes, freedom isn't free. So what does that mean?

Well, it doesn't just apply in the military sense, though the soldiers serving our country certainly make huge sacrifices to protect us. The saying also applies to the fact that every society depends on taxes to pay for community services, like police departments, social programs, and government agencies that do everything from gathering intelligence to making sure your food isn't full of disease. These services are to the benefit of everyone, and for the most part, you should feel proud that your future tax dollars will serve the greater good. But paying taxes isn't where your responsibilities as an American stop. Even if you are free to do as you please, you owe it to yourself and your fellow Americans to do a few things above and beyond paying taxes.

The best way for you to understand your responsibilities as an American is to combine the above saying with another popular gem: "Nothing is free." You see, while America does afford each of us the opportunity to pursue nearly any line of work/education/lifestyle we want, our actions still have consequences that affect others. Whether your behavior is good or bad, someone else is affected. Other Americans are not "free" from the fallout of your behavior.

So what does this mean for you? What can you do as a young American to make sure that your actions are not detrimental to the overall health of the nation? You can do many things, but first let's discuss why you should be taking this section of the book seriously.

Our nation does indeed celebrate the individual, some more deserving than others. We are encouraged to express ourselves and to carve a path that is unique to us as individuals. We celebrate those in our past who have broken away from the group to forge new frontiers and to try new things. These are our positive role models, the people who have stood up above the crowd to create positive changes: Martin Luther King Jr., Neil Armstrong, Lewis and Clark, Amelia Earhart, etc.

Our nation has had a fantastic history of positive progression because of these people. We've also moved forward because of the collective will of our people. During WWII and following September 11, our nation showed the world that we can come together to accomplish phenomenal things. We could set aside our differences and forge through challenges that might break other nations.

We believe as a nation that the individual person—whether acting alone or as part of a group—can make a change. We can affect the experiences of other people by making the decision to do something positive. Unfortunately, the inverse is true: we can negatively affect others if we choose to do so. So when you think about what to do with your life and the decisions you should make on a daily basis, don't believe that no one is noticing; don't assume that your actions have nothing to do with anyone else.

You do have responsibilities to other people. And you do have responsibilities to your country. The freedom to enjoy your life as you please is a freedom protected by civil libertarians, soldiers, police, legislators, and more. You can reward their efforts by being a productive contributor to society. No matter what you choose to do with your life, there are a few "musts" in being a positive influence for your country.

Don't Expect Anyone to Give You Anything

That may sound harsh, but think of it this way. You probably have athletes or celebrities you admire; it's only natural to look up to those that have experienced a great deal of success. And chances are that some of these people are wealthy. Let us look at two people from different disciplines as examples: Tiger Woods and Oprah Winfrey. Both are wealthy and both are very visible figures in our society, so a lot of people are paying attention to what they do.

Now looking at the amounts of money earned by both Winfrey and Woods, you're probably thinking, "Man, it would be awesome if I had just a tenth of that.

Couldn't they just give me, like, a million bucks? They wouldn't even notice it was gone." And while this is a nice fantasy, you don't actually expect Tiger Woods to show up at your front door with a suitcase full of cash. You don't feel entitled to the money. So why do some people feel entitled to money from their government?

Most expect money or feel entitled to money because they pay taxes. They say, "I pay my taxes, why shouldn't I get part of the bailout?" And maybe they have a point. But there are also people who don't work, who still expect a helping hand, and most of the time they get it. But let's look at this situation a little closer and see whether or not these people actually deserve money from the government any more than they would from Tiger Woods.

First of all, most of the income taxes paid in this country are paid by wealthy individuals. The amount of taxes paid every year by Berkshire Hathaway, the massive company helmed by Warren Buffet. Every year, his company pays billions in tax income. In fact, in 2006, before the financial collapse, they paid $4.4 billion in taxes. So even if your parents and their friends paid $20,000 each that same year, Buffet's company would have paid for the equivalent of 220,000 people. That's as many people as attend the Indianapolis 500 each year!

Second, many of the people taking government handouts are not working or haven't paid taxes in years. They contribute little to the overall welfare of the nation in a financial sense. Imagine you belonged to a club at school, a club planning a trip to Europe. You work all year to raise the money needed for the ten members of your club. Through bake sales and car washes and private donations, you're able to raise the money needed. And the two weeks before the trip, your club president announces that ten new members are being admitted to the club and that they will be allowed to partake in the trip to Europe. Only, there isn't enough money for twenty people, just ten. So nobody gets to go because you have to be fair to everyone. Everyone deserves the same benefits.

While these examples can't explain all the issues associated with government handouts, they make the point that you shouldn't look at the government as an entity that owes you something. If you've worked hard and paid your taxes, then you should receive assistance from social security and other programs, but don't believe that because you've paid taxes the amount of money you receive should be endless.

Work Hard in School

This seems like such a clichéd saying. "Work hard in school and eat your fruits and vegetables." You might hear your grandmother say something like this when she's trying to get you to improve your grades. So why does it matter how hard you work in school? Shouldn't you have the right to flunk out if you want? Aren't you the only one truly paying the price? Not by a long shot.

People who drop out of school are almost sure to end up in low-paying jobs for life. And while that is a steep price to pay for the individual, the reality is that when the economy goes south, low-wage workers are the first ones to be laid off. When they're laid off, they end up needing assistance from the government. That assistance comes out of the pockets of other Americans who've worked hard to attain good work that pays well.

We're not referring to the skilled laborers who've learned a craft. We're referring to the kids who had the potential to learn a skilled craft or who had the option of going to college but chose not to. They may believe that their inaction affects no one other than themselves, but they couldn't be farther from the truth.

It's not hard to believe that a lot of your peers don't value school. There's a saying that is appropriate for many of these kids: "Teens can't see around corners." You may have also heard this saying as "Youth is wasted on the young." When you get older, you start to realize how much the early part of your life laid the groundwork for where you've ended up. The decisions you made in high school affected which college you attended (if at all) and the decisions you made post-high school (whether in college or elsewhere) have dictated what you do for a living, how much money you make, and where you live.

You may not be able to see this if you are not aware of the consequences of your actions. If you could, you'd realize how important it is for you to dedicate yourself. By applying yourself in school, you help yourself to succeed. You can stand on your own and you can contribute expertise to the workforce. If you don't think your own expertise and imagination can have an effect, think again. Every person's energy and enthusiasm add to the greater economy and its output. The world is a great deal larger than your high school, and our nation is now competing with others for economic footholds. That means we need all the help we can get.

Secure Work and Support Yourself and Your Family

Getting a good education means you end up being in demand as an employee. You have something to offer employers, and so you are never without work. You can support yourself and your family and contribute to the tax base.

As a self-supporting worker, you contribute a great deal to the economy. You'll be a consumer of large goods, such as a home or car. You'll provide others with jobs as an employer or by hiring people to do work around your house or on your car. When you buy luxury goods, you'll be contributing to the jobs sectors in those industries.

Being self-supportive means not only standing on your own but also helping others to stand tall. Each person, no matter how much of an "individual" they are, is connected to others in an economical sense. Unless you're a complete miser, your money goes out into the general economy, even if it's just for paying bills. That money helps to support others in their jobs. Even better, you're supporting people whom you choose to support. Your taxes are already being used to support people, so you might as well support people who provide you with products and services you need and want.

No Money, No Babies

The affordability of a family may seem like a strange thing for a young person to be thinking about. After all, you're a child in many ways and are being supported (hopefully) by your own parents. If all goes well, you'll have children when you're good and ready and not before. Unfortunately, many people put little thought into the realities of parenthood and believe that love is all they need to raise a child. Love is a good start, but as any responsible parent will tell you, parenthood can cost a lot of money.

You have to pay for diapers, medications, doctor's visits, formula, a crib, changing table, stroller, car seat, and on and on. That's not to mention the maternity clothes and the medical costs of having the child in the first place. If you're being healthy about the process, you're going to have ultrasounds and doctor's visits about once a month. You're going to need tests and more tests if something is wrong.

Most parents gladly pay for these things because they understand it's part of the process of having a healthy child and providing for her/him. They know these costs in advance and make a decision to go ahead with parenthood because they want a family. But as stated earlier in this chapter, some people don't think ahead. They either get pregnant by accident or get pregnant on purpose with no real way of supporting a family.

Because our actions always have consequences, these same people end up needing help providing for their children. They go on to welfare and take part in multiple social programs designed to help parents and children who are truly in need. It's a selfish act and one that is completely preventable. Contraceptives are easy to obtain, and even though it's sometimes hard to decide to use them in the heat of the moment, it's a decision that saves all of us the negative consequences of people who have children they can't afford to support.

Government Ain't Your Baby Daddy

One of the key areas of responsibility in anyone's life is that of raising children. Without the support of their parents, children are helpless. They need around-the-clock care from the time they are born until they are old enough to be left alone. Caring for kids is a major, major task. And yet millions of American men and boys have walked away from it.

It used to be the case in this country, and in others, that if you got a girl pregnant, you were going to be forced to marry her. These weddings were often called "shotgun weddings" because it was assumed the groom walked down the aisle under the careful watch of the bride's father, sometimes with a shotgun in his hand. Fatherhood was taken seriously, and if a man had a child with a woman and then abandoned them, he was seen as an outcast, someone who couldn't be trusted and who wasn't responsible enough to take care of even the basic needs of his family.

Today, more than twenty-five million American children live in fatherless homes, according to the National Fatherhood Initiative. That's a huge percentage of American children being raised without a father figure, someone to provide a solid role model for male behavior. Now you may think that a man's relationship with his girlfriend/wife/fling is his business alone, but our country spends billions every year on single mothers who might not need government assistance if the fathers of their children would provide financial and emotional support.

Here are some statistics to demonstrate just how costly this problem is dollarwise, not to mention emotionally and psychologically. These statistics come from a study performed by the University of Virginia and the DePaul University School of Public Service, titled *The One Hundred Billion Dollar Man: The Annual Public Costs of Father Absence*:

- Between 1960 and 2006, the number of children living in single-mother families went from eight percent to 23.3 percent. Currently, 34 percent of children live without their biological father.
- In 2003, it was found that about 40 percent of single-mother families lived in poverty, compared to 8.8 percent of father-present families.
- In 2006, the federal government spent $99.8 billion providing assistance to father-absent families. This assistance fell under several programs:
  o Earned Income Tax Credit
  o Temporary Assistance for Needy Families (TANF)
  o Child support enforcement efforts
  o Food and nutrition programs, such as WIC

- o   Housing programs
- o   Medicaid
- o   The State Children's Health Insurance Plan (SCHIP)

These statistics reveal a deeply disturbing trend in personal responsibility in the country. In just four decades, the men of this country decided, and were allowed, to abandon many of the children they father. That demonstrates just how quickly the fabric of a nation can be torn apart when the individual stops being mature enough to live up to obligations.

The cost to the federal government is going to increase in the coming years, and you can bet that the $100 billion being spent in 2006 was just a drop in the bucket compared to what will be spent as President Obama increases funding to social programs. But what about the fathers? Why aren't they paying the price for all this? And why did they engage in such risky behavior in the first place?

It seems that the shift in the country from "Work hard and accept responsibility for your actions" to "It's not your fault, your circumstances were difficult, and no one told you any better" has left a lot of mothers caring for children they can't afford. But the mothers are not innocent victims in all this.

Sex is an act between two people, and when that sex is anything but safe sex, the consequences are on both of the people involved. The girls and women of this country are not taking responsibility for their own bodies. They are allowing men and boys to convince them that unprotected sex is okay and that any child produced from the act will be taken care of. The bar has been set so low for accountability that when a man goes back on his word and walks out on a girl he's gotten pregnant, we simply call him a "bum" and move on helping the mother and child. But why are women allowing these irresponsible bums to get near them in the first place?

In previous decades, a man was revered when he stood up for his actions and did the right thing, even if it cost him personally. And there were enough role models out there for men to follow and for women to learn from. A girl could look at her father going to work every day and providing for his family, and understand that his behavior was emblematic of how a man should act. The daughter of a man like that wouldn't accept a partner whose behavior was any less responsible.

Slowly, the liberal establishment in this country eased the definition of responsible when they decided to implement the "It's not your fault" culture we have today. You see, no one is to blame for their behavior; the "system" is to blame. If a girl gets pregnant, it's because she has low self-esteem and because no one taught her to respect herself. If a guy gets a girl pregnant and then runs out on the situation, it's because he was raised without a role model and because a young man can't be expected to handle such an overwhelming task as raising a child.

The problem with this attitude is that it is the parents' fault. They are to blame for getting pregnant, and they should be responsible for caring for their children. But these young mothers have come to expect assistance from the government, as have the fathers. They assume that if there is no money earner in the house, welfare and other programs will swoop in to make up for the difference.

Can you imagine if the federal government started phasing out social programs to support single mothers? The outcry from the public would be tremendous. People would be crying from the hills that the government was targeting the poor and was abandoning the children of the nation. Why should the poor be held to any lower a standard of personal responsibility than the middle or upper class are? If a middle-class man gets a middle-class woman pregnant and then leaves her to fend for herself, there is no government help. If she earns enough to pay for day care, her financial burden is her own to bear.

Essentially, what the government is saying to these young men and women (and not all of them are young, some women continue acting stupidly well into their thirties) is that they are not smart enough to make good decisions because they are poor. The government is treating these people as ignorant peasants that need help because they don't know any better. But that's a lie. Poor people are just as capable of making the decision to have safe sex as anyone else is. It's just that the bar of responsibility has been lowered so much for their economic category that they feel justified in not caring about consequences.

In order to fix this problem, our country needs to go away from social programs that reward stupid decisions. If you get pregnant because you had unprotected sex, you should be prepared to live with the consequences of that decision, including the possibility of becoming pregnant. Our country would do well to focus more on prevention than on handouts. Sex education should be more realistic, and it should be made clear to students around the country that the safety net of the federal government will not be there to protect them. Our government though, especially under the Democrats, is not likely to support prevention with such measures. That would mean angry voters, and that's something no politician wants to see.

Even the anger that voters would express would be symbolic. It would represent the entitlement that many people feel toward social programs. Many of these mothers and fathers expect help from the government even if they haven't paid taxes a day in their lives. Don't end up like these fatherless families. Stand up for what you've done and make smart decisions so that you don't become part of a culture that believes the government is the baby daddy.

Strive to Be Good at Your Work

As you saw in the previous chapter section "The Lost Workday," not enough people strive to be good at their jobs. Many Americans view their jobs as inconveniences that they have to tend to while waiting for the weekend to come along. The economic collapse of 2008 changed some people's minds on this topic, but there are a lot of people who still view every job as a temporary distraction that is keeping them from enjoying their lives. They are at their jobs simply to collect a check, and asking them to do more than "get by" would be too much of a burden for them to handle.

Most jobs aren't fun; in fact, many of them are downright miserable. If you've ever seen the TV show *Dirty Jobs*, you've seen that many Americans spend their days doing work that is hot, miserable, low paying, and physically demanding. But that doesn't mean these workers don't strive to be good at what they do.

Whether you decide to be an accountant or a mailman, strive to be the best you can at what you do. Even if a job is temporary or part-time, do it well. There are many reasons to do so:

Legacy: If you're young, you probably haven't thought much about how you want people to remember you after you've moved on from a job or school. But the way that people remember us has a lot to do with the kinds of recommendations and references we can get. It also has to do with our ability to network in order to find better jobs or to secure future business for our companies. Do you really want your fellow students or fellow workers to remember you as someone who didn't show up to work? Someone who never bothered to do their work? There is a stigma attached to people who don't do good work, even if they never realize it.

Opportunity. When it comes, the time to go for that dream job, you'll be up against other workers who want to enjoy the same benefits and same pay as you do. There will be competition between workers who have similar backgrounds and who possess similar skills. The ones that will move ahead of the pack though are the ones that have gone the extra step to improve their abilities. Businesses call these work sills "competencies," and they value people that have developed them. In today's economy, employers can afford to be choosy. They can select only the most skilled workers for employment, and trust me when I tell you this: you do not want to be the guy with the thin résumé. In addition, most employers will contact your previous places of employment to ask about your work habits. Do you really want your former boss telling your prospective employer that you wasted your potential?

Skills development. It's believed that most Americans will change *careers* multiple times during their working lives, not just jobs. That means learning new skills and using your previous skills to add value to your new career. The more skills you develop as a worker, the more tools you'll have to help you in managing a career change. Some skills, such as computer skills or the ability to communicate both verbally and in written form, can transfer between dozens of careers. Learning these skills will put you in a position to transition quickly into better-paying (or simply hiring) careers.

Self-discipline. You've probably seen coworkers or peers who simply couldn't be bothered to put in the effort. Whether it was a school project or a mundane task at work, they went through the motions as though they were being tortured. A lot of people act this way, and as you get out into the career field, you'll find more of them than you could have ever thought possible. These people haven't ever learned to discipline themselves. It's easy to be engaged in doing something you like to do. You've probably never met anyone who said they had trouble focusing on watching television or on relaxing in a lounge chair. But plenty of people have trouble forcing themselves to do things that are less entertaining, particularly at work. Most of life, however, is taken up by work or "maintenance" tasks. Without any self-discipline, these areas of life suffer. By making yourself work hard at every job you have, you'll learn your own methods of working and how you can spur yourself on to do great things.

Take the Credit; Take the Blame

I'll bet if you surveyed your friends about their willingness to accept responsibility for their failures you'd find that most say they are, and they're not alone. Most people when asked about responsibility would say they are responsible people, that they accept blame as well as credit. But they'd be lying.

If you have siblings, you know what I mean. People start lying at a very young age. When something is broken around the house, fingers begin pointing in all directions. It seems no one person did. You see, it was someone else. This "someone else" is responsible for almost every mistake made in the world, and it seems he or she is never around.

Blaming other people for your mistakes for failures is natural. No one wants to face negative consequences. No one wants to appear a failure or a screw-up. People seek to preserve their own egos and well-beings, and so they naturally look for culprits to ease some of the blame they might feel for a mistake. In the end though—and if you consider the example of your siblings again—laying blame on others rarely works for long.

If you make it a habit to blame others at work, you'll soon find that no one respects you. If you blame others at school, you'll soon find you have few friends you can count on. The negative consequences you seek to avoid are simply manifested in another form of failure: a failure of character.

People with weak characters are prone to lying anyways, so it's not uncommon to see defendants in court lying about everything. They don't want to go to jail no matter how guilty they are. But you don't want to end up like those people, suspected of lying at every turn. As stated above, you'll soon find you have few friends.

So what do you gain from pointing the finger at yourself? What you get is a chance to learn, a chance to stand on your own two feet, and a chance to advance yourself as a person. People who take responsibility for their successes and failures are looked to as leaders and are relied upon in jobs of greater responsibility and greater pay.

So what does this have to do with being a good American? A nation is only as good as its people. If you don't think your behavior has anything to do with the overall health of the country, you're mistaken. Every single person has a responsibility to be as responsible as they can be.

Here's an example: Take a look at your neighborhood. Do the people in it take responsibility for keeping their homes clean and in good condition? If you live in an apartment building, do all of the utilities work and does your superintendent take pride in how the building looks?

If you answered yes to this question, you probably live in a nice neighborhood or one that's improving. That's how neighborhoods get better: the people in the neighborhood take responsibility for their own piece of it. The same goes for the larger city and the nation itself. Do your part. Do what you're supposed to do, and you'll be contributing more than you can know.

Not a lot of discussion goes into personal responsibility in high schools anymore. Most of the focus now is on our personal rights as Americans. And while some school districts require that students perform a certain number of volunteer hours before graduating, the lesson is a superficial one.

Being made to volunteer is not being taught responsibility. If you really want to learn personal responsibility, then do the little things. Don't cheat on tests, don't skip class, or pick on other kids. Stand up for what's right, and admit when you've screwed up. Carry this behavior over to home, and admit to your parents when you've made a mistake; they'll appreciate it.

Learn English

There is nothing wrong with being bilingual. It is an asset and one that will help you find work when you move beyond school. But it is important that you adopt English and learn to speak it as well as possible.

First, it will mean a great deal in advancing your education. English is the language of business in our nation, and to know it well means to have access to jobs and opportunities that might elude someone who struggles with the language. The fact of the matter is that image counts in business. Someone who struggles to communicate in English will be seen as wrong for so many of the jobs in corporate America, including sales, communications, public relations, and more.

Second, adopting English as your native language allows for broader access in a social sense as well. Too many times in our country, the "native" English speakers look at immigrants as being a nuisance, even if they're legal. That divide should not be allowed to separate us. By being able to communicate, we can bridge that divide by showing each other the benefits of having multiple cultures feeding the American experience. Imagine being able to ask someone about their native country. The opportunities to learn in these instances would be magnificent.

Third, there exists in our country a bigotry that assumes that anyone who doesn't speak English is less intelligent than someone who does. Some Americans are surprised to learn that engineers, doctors, and architects exist in places like Mexico or El Salvador. Overcoming these prejudices is something that falls to both Americans and immigrants. By being able to communicate effectively, the educated immigrant can show his or her new countrymen the wealth of "brain power" that comes into this country as part of the immigrant influx. Without effective English, many of these educated workers are left working menial jobs. Their skills and expertise are going to waste because they can't communicate their value to employers.

You Are an American First

There is a great difference between celebrating your heritage and putting your native country first over America. The United States provides a great deal of freedom to its residence: freedom of the press, freedom of religion, freedom of political affiliation. And all it asks for in return is loyalty.

Loyalty, of course, does not mean zero dissent. It simply means that when it comes to claiming a nationality and supporting a nation, you choose the United

States above all others. Keep your heritage, celebrate your roots, but embrace the fact that you're in the United States and are a part of something great.

Each person has to find his way as an American. The road to figuring out what kind of person you want to be can be difficult, and that holds true for your role as an American. Making the right choices and upholding your responsibilities can mean personal sacrifice, from obeying traffic laws to giving your life for your nation. In the end, though, our country will be better off if you decide to follow even a few of the steps laid out in this chapter.

The Responsibility to Vote

If you don't have it now, you will soon have the right to vote. Exercising your right to vote is the greatest thing you can do as an American. It is what allows the peaceful exchange of power. It is the legacy that George Washington left us, and it is the legacy that you must continue today. Your vote is powerful. Don't be swayed by movie stars and by what the popular thing is to do. Learn the facts for yourself and make an educated choice.

The American dream is one in which Americans and new legal immigrants alike can assimilate into our society, play by the rules, and can prosper like no other citizens in the world can. That is why millions of people come to this country: to live the American dream.

In November of 2008, the United States voted for a president who holds this American dream in disdain. Who villainizes success and feels that the government must control all aspects of your life. You cannot create wealth through government jobs, and you cannot create wealth by taking it from people who have obtained it through hard work. Wealth must be created through jobs, freedom, financial responsibility, and low taxes.

We cannot succeed by borrowing money from other countries that we cannot afford to pay back, stealing money from those who have worked hard, and burdening our society by promising rights which the government cannot grant or sustain. We have learned a valuable lesson in the last few years. The principles of small central government and freedom is what made America great and is what will make America great in the end.

Charity does not start with the government; instead, charity starts with the individual who has the freedom to choose to support causes in which he or she believes in. We cannot trust the inefficient big government to provide for our neighbors or us. People do not flock to socialist and communist countries for their freedoms and opportunities. Those countries are failing all over the world, and people are fleeing them. Don't let this country fundamentally transform into another failing communist regime. We are at a crossroads in time where powerful factions are flying our plane in the wrong direction. It is up to each of us to put this country back on the right course.

As a voter, focus your efforts on people who uphold the ideal that hard work can lead to success. Vote for those that see the successful and the wealthy as exemplars and will do the right thing for the country even though it may not make a lot of people who are expecting handouts happy.

CHAPTER 8

REPRESENTATION WITHOUT TAXATION

When the founders of the United States decided to break away from the United Kingdom, one of their motivating factors was unfair taxation by the British. The colonists were being taxed on all sorts of items, including stamps and tea, without any direct representation in the British parliament. The founders felt it was unfair that they be taxed by people who gave them no say in how high the taxes were or even if the taxes were fair to begin with. It was taxation without representation.

Our nation currently faces a dilemma that is quite the opposite. Everyone of voting age in our country can vote provided they aren't a felon, though some in the government are trying to change this. If you're eighteen and you register with your county registrar, you can go to the polls and have your voice heard. The problem with this is that many, many Americans, as many as 48 percent, aren't paying federal income taxes *at all* and are still allowed to vote. It is *representation without taxation*.

Consider your school basketball team. The coaches and the players have invested a lot of time, hard work, and resources into making their team the best it can be. Now imagine that the rest of the student body can select who plays and who doesn't play and what plays are called on the court. They have put no effort into the team, and they are not part of the team. However, they are part of the school, and they can all share in the pride of the school. But they shouldn't have a say in how the team is run.

Extending voting rights in federal elections to people who don't pay federal **income** taxes is no different. Our nation is being guided, in part, by people who contribute nothing to the overall pot of money the federal government uses to pay for vital (and also completely unnecessary) services. Just as you wouldn't want someone invading your Facebook page and changing all the information, you also wouldn't want someone voting in a politician who is going to raise your taxes and spend as though there is no tomorrow. Well, many of the people who voted for just such a politician (Barack Obama) were nontaxpayers.

These nontaxpayers are not vested in the country's economy. They contribute nothing in the way of tax dollars, but they are still given an equal voice when it comes to picking a politician. It's like having a club in school that is subject to the desires of nonmembers. It would be as if these same nonmembers ask the club to raise funds for a cause that they support, not a cause that is in best interest of the club. And so it is that many taxpayers are starting to resent the choices of nontaxpayers. We want to make it clear at this point, however, that this does not apply to everyone who is not currently paying federal income taxes. Retirees with limited incomes are exempt because they have paid into the system for years.

Here's another example: If a church decides that they are going to give money to a certain charity, they have the right to do so. And if ten years down the road they decide they want to stop giving it to that charity, the charity does not get a say in where the church's money goes instead. People receiving handouts should not have a say in where the federal government's money goes. Everyone who wants a say must contribute to the system.

So why is it that these noncontributors are able to wield influence and keep their votes? Why is it that these people are being listened to more than business owners who pay a tremendous amount of tax are? Why are business owners and their employees being treated as the bad guys?

The reason is simple: Progressives appeal to the nontaxpayer because the Progressives want to stay in office and they know they can count on those people who accept government handouts. Why wouldn't you vote for someone who gives you something for nothing? The nontaxpayers in this country are people at the very bottom of the financial totem pole. That doesn't mean that all poor people should be denied the right to vote. But those that subsist entirely on welfare and that make little effort to find employment should be denied a voice in voting.

Progressives love welfare. They love social programs that give money away and that make people feel supported by their government. The people on these programs know which party is in favor of massive social programs. They know which party will keep increasing these programs regardless of the expense. And they know that all the party wants in return is a vote. The party members, like all politicians, want to stay in power. They stay in power by "buying" the votes of people on social welfare programs.

It may seem harsh to deny an American their right to vote. But this ban on voting is a statement to those Americans who believe that paying taxes is something they don't need to be a part of. This is aimed at Americans who feel offended when their government stops giving them handouts and starts demanding sacrifice. Many Americans simply believe they shouldn't have to pay taxes. They believe that their government should be there to pick them up and help them out no matter how poor the decisions they have made.

The irony is that the same people who "look out" for the lower classes and give them handouts full of other people's money are really just using the lower classes. They want them to stay dependent and to keep voting for them. Short-term assistance may be beneficial, but welfare is a control mechanism to keep poor people dependent. Now you know the truth about government handouts, the government should do all it can to allow jobs to be created (lower taxes to allow growth for business), not create government dependency.

It is shocking how many of our fellow citizens immediately blame the government for their failures and who harbor resentment toward the government when they don't receive more of a handout than they are already receiving. Participation in our nation's electoral process should be earned, not given. It's time that Americans learned that this nation does not operate automatically and that the freedoms we enjoy here are not free.

"But I'm too young to vote. Why should I care?"

If you're in high school, you're too young to vote, and so you're probably asking why you should care about any of this. Why should you worry if other people want to vote? You probably don't pay taxes either, and so you can't imagine what all the fuss is about. But thinking that voting is someone else's problem is shortsighted.

Think about the average politician in your mind? What kind of image comes to mind when you think of the word politician? Probably someone old. And you wouldn't be too far off. Most national-level politicians are older. Why? Because young people of voting age don't vote. They simply do not vote on a scale that will matter to most national elections.

Young people often feel disconnected from politics because they don't see a face like theirs on the national stage. And they don't believe that most of the issues that matter to them are being addressed by politicians. And they would be right for the most part because politicians cater to those who vote.

If you just look closely though, you'll see that even if you are too young to vote, your life is being shaped by the people in office—the same people who will likely be in office when it is your turn to vote. The schools you go to, the taxes your parents pay, the amount of tax on cell phones, the rules regarding Internet censorship, the rights of teenagers under the law . . . all these things are decided by politicians.

Voting has become passé in our country because most people have been content with the economy and the rights we enjoy as citizens. But as the economy continues to bubble and burst and as spending by the government increases dramatically, more people are going to get involved. More people are going to decide to vote. The question of who gets to vote is an important one and will become more important to you on a personal level as you get older. You'll realize soon that many of the people politicians pander to are contributing virtually nothing to the well-being of the nation. And yet these people are selecting politicians that care little for fiscal responsibility or long-term thinking.

When our nation finally faces its massive debts, we as a people will be forced to make some very difficult decisions about what we spend our money on. By that time, you'll likely have children of your own in school and you'll have a job and a house and you'll be paying taxes. And all of a sudden, you'll realize that educational cuts and increased social spending and a host of other consequences were caused by the politicians we have in office today. That's why voting is so important, and that's why it should be a privilege that is earned.

Chapter 9

Managing Money

Starting in early 2010, school systems in Britain were required to begin giving their pupils lessons on managing debt. It was a long-overdue move made by their government and a move still not made by our government. Our students need lessons on money management probably more than students in Britain do, but as yet, they aren't on the curriculum. Our students are taught about the Revolutionary War, which they should be, but even basics of debt management are not made a priority by our schools and government leaders.

So here is a primer on debt (and its sometimes synonym, credit).

Debt is borrowed money. Plain and simple. That's a concept many of you reading this book won't have experienced firsthand unless you've borrowed a few bucks from a friend to buy a soda. But your parents are dealing with debt every day and that's because if they own a home or car, they likely had to borrow money to pay for it. But they couldn't just borrow the money and pay it back. They have to pay interest, which is where most people run into trouble with debt.

You see, debt really has two parts: *principal*, the amount you need to borrow, and *interest*, which is what you'll be charged to borrow the money. This is called a finance charge, and it's how lenders make their money. They agree to lend you money that you need, but in return they require that you pay them a percentage of the money on top of what you owe. You may have seen loan sharks in movies talking about the "vig" or the "juice." These evil men beat up their clients if they don't pay what they owe. Well, banks and mortgage lenders don't beat up their clients if they fail to pay, but they do spread the word in the form of a poor credit rating that the borrower is unreliable. That makes life really tough for the borrower if he or she ever wants to borrow money in the future.

Principal

Principal is a funny thing. If down the road you want to buy a car, you'll likely haggle with the salesman over how much you want to pay for the car. As an example, the salesman wants to get $24,000 for the car, but you only want to pay $22,000. That's the principal of what you'll need to borrow, assuming you don't have any money in your pocket. Most people would be thrilled if they convinced the salesman to sell them the car at their reduced rate. And in the years of 2008 and 2009, there were deals like this to be had. But most people won't bother to calculate the "true" cost of the vehicle after they've paid both principal and interest.

Calculating interest isn't fun. It's a pain in the neck actually, but there are myriad online "payment" calculators that will show you just how much your house or car will cost you when you're all done paying for it. And for the uninitiated, the results can be shocking. For example: let's take that car you've just bought for $22,000. If you don't provide anything as a down payment and you agree to pay back the loan over five years, with a relatively low interest rate of 7.12 percent and a 7 percent sales tax, you will end up paying $28,047 for your vehicle. That means that in exchange for borrowing the $23,540 (the $22,000 cost of the car plus sales tax), you pay the lender $4,507.

But wait, it gets more complicated (and more dangerous) when you borrow money at an interest rate that is not "fixed" or the same for the life of the loan. Some lenders will lend you money at what is called a "variable" rate. This variable rate means that the interest you pay can change over time, often getting more and more expensive during the life of the loan.

Credit Cards

Credit cards offer a particularly dangerous form of debt. The credit card companies are able to offer money with terms that would make a loan shark blush. Most companies can adjust rates for even a single late payment, often doubling the amount of interest owed. On top of this, they can charge exorbitant late fees and even offer cards that have introductory rates, which entice consumers who are too distracted to notice that the rate disappears after six months, replaced by one that can be well over 20 percent and even as high as 35 percent.

College freshmen are particularly susceptible to the debt trap because they are unaware of all this. They see credit cards as an easy way to live a life of independence that they would otherwise be unable to afford. Of course, they rarely examine the fine print on credit card contracts and so overlook the outrageous interest rate they are being charged. It's a hard lesson to learn and one this section is decided to prevent. Pay attention to any contract you sign, and think long and hard about what it will take to pay back any money you owe.

Good Debt

Not all debt is bad. Business owners borrow money through short-term loans to cover the cost of payroll. They also borrow money to invest in new equipment or expansion of the business. Homeowners often borrow money to reinvest in the home in the form of improvements that will increase the sales value (at least that's the hope).

In the case of young students, good debt can come in the form of an investment in education. Student loans are often needed to pay for a university education, but it pays off in the long run because a college education is a great starting point for securing more lucrative and in-demand career paths.

How Debt Relates to Your Country

We've spent a lot of time in this book discussing how the government is spending much more money than they make. This money, of course, is borrowed money (debt); and so it must be paid back with interest. You can help make your nation a more sound financial institution by securing your own finances. You will avoid needing subsidized social programs to support you, easing the burden on the taxpayers of the nation. It may not seem like much for one person to keep him or herself afloat, but it makes a huge difference if thousands or millions of Americans make the same decisions. Managing your debt is one place to start building a secure financial future.

CHAPTER 10

CAREER MANAGEMENT

If you're still in high school (or even college), you probably have no idea what you want to do as a career. In fact, your parents may feel the same way. That's because people often "fall into" careers by virtue of their interests or by whichever job seems to best suit their skills and personality. As an example: few people graduate from high-school thinking they would like be an actuary at an insurance company, assessing the risk of different life insurance policies, but there are people doing that job every day.

As you progress through college or vocational school, you'll likely encounter subjects that intrigue you. Even in high school, you'll have hobbies or areas of study that seem to better suit the way you think. Some people consider themselves "math" oriented or "English" oriented. Identifying your strong suits is a good start toward identifying a career path.

Some people will encourage you to choose a career that involves one of your hobbies or passions. But the reality is that this isn't always possible. It's ideal to have a job you like and that you are passionate about, but it is *necessary* to have a job that supports you and your family. This is something most teachers won't come out and tell you that most people work jobs they don't particularly care for but that pay the bills.

If you're going to be a responsible citizen, one that works hard enough to avoid needing financial assistance, then you need to consider a pragmatic approach to career choices. Some of us simply have passions or hobbies in areas that don't pay. What is most important is that once you select a path, you work hard at staying in-demand.

In American schools we talk about competition from students in developing nations and we talk about what to wear to an interview, but rarely do we speak about fighting for a job. Most job openings draw dozens of applications. Some of these applications are from people overqualified for the job. These people are likely having trouble finding work, and so they apply for anything available. Other applications are from people grossly unqualified for the work. In today's economy, employers can afford to pick and choose whom they hire. Do you think the overqualified or the underqualified candidate will get the position?

Being in-demand means staying constantly qualified and maybe even overqualified for your particular field of work. Some people believe that once they reach a certain position of seniority, they no longer need to stay hungry. But career development involves lifelong education. That is why one of the major tasks your teachers have is showing you *how* to learn. School isn't just about memorizing hundreds of dates and names from wars a thousand years ago. It is a chance to develop your learning tools so that when you get into the career world, you have the discipline and the ability to constantly learn new skills. If you remain stagnant in any career, others will pass you by.

Make Your Education a Real Springboard

The time you spend in school is really the beginning of your career successes or failures. Most students will only understand the importance of school much later in life usually because they regret not taking it more seriously. Many a college student spends more time partying than learning. These people still earn degrees, but have they taken advantage of the resources a university offers? Probably not.

If you are a student, you have but one job: to learn as much as you can. You have tremendous resources at your disposal in the form of professors, libraries, tutors, research projects, and more. If you want to be an architect, spend the time you have in school to really learn what the job involves. Take it upon yourself to be curious and to learn more than you are required to learn. Most people study for tests while they're in school; few study for careers.

If you are in college, try your best to secure an internship so that you can experience a career firsthand. Many students find out through their internships that they have chosen a career path that doesn't suit them. It's better to find out while you're still in school than to find out after taking your first job. Learn as much as you can about the actual application of your learning so that you understand why you are attending classes and taking tests. You've probably heard classmates saying, "Why am I learning this? I'll never use it." That may be true for some material, but with a clear picture in your mind of what your career will involve, you can stay motivated to learn new things.

Network!

The Internet has become a crutch for many job seekers, but research has shown that most jobs are acquired through personal contacts and not through an online application process. If you've heard the expression "It's all about who you know," then you get some idea of why networking is so powerful a tool. Of course, there are no networking classes in school. It is a skill that requires real-world practice and a sense of social decorum. You can't just come out and ask someone for a job, but you can call on your contacts to see if they have open positions, which you can then apply for.

Social networking sites have made this process somewhat easier. Business-specific sites such as LinkedIn are providing prospective employees the chance to build a network of friends and acquaintances. These people are "at the ready," just in case a member of the site is looking for a job. But the reality is that you need to meet face-to-face with people. The expression "It's all about who you know," may have some truth to it, but when you are looking for a job and competing against thousands of other workers, the expression should read: "It's about who knows you."

Because networking is so valuable, the process should never stop for you no matter how secure you feel in your job. There is always the chance of a business going under or handing out layoffs. You need to always keep your options open. The government will be there to help you with unemployment, but that doesn't last forever despite President Obama's efforts to make it that way. Taking responsibility for your career means planning for the possibility that you will lose your job. Networking is a great way to do that.

Nobody Owes You Anything, Even If You Did Graduate College

A college degree does not entitle you to anything and neither does a master's degree or PhD. There are thousands of students every year who earn master's degrees and thousands more who earn undergraduate degrees. You are not special in that regard, unless you finished near the top of your class in an in-demand area of study. But in general, you are competing against other candidates with at least undergraduate degrees.

Prior to the financial collapse, there was an epidemic of young workers feeling entitled to management positions or to special treatment by their bosses. Many grew up being told by their parents that they were special, and when they hit the reality of the job market and were assigned lower-level or even menial tasks, they couldn't handle it. Many changed jobs frequently, looking for a position that better coddled them. Don't be that person!

You will have to pay your dues. You will have to work hard. You will have to do what your boss says to do. You are not going to be treated as special until you prove that you are indeed special. Your positions in your organization will be hard earned and probably far from safe. This is the reality of the job market. Make your own success. We guarantee that if you work hard and show up every day, on time, that you'll be head and shoulders above many of your peers.

Bosses like nothing more than an employee who cares. They like commitment. They hate entitlement. Most managers work hard, and they have positions of responsibility and pressure. They don't particularly like young graduates coming into the company and demanding special treatment. Show your employer that you understand how to earn your keep and then apply those same work lessons to your life. Even if your government thinks hard work is antiquated, you don't have to think the same way.

How Career Management Relates to Your Country

It is true that achievers are punished by the current government. If you are particularly successful in a lucrative field, you will soon find yourself a target of the taxman. As disturbing as this reality is, it is something to be changed in the political sphere. As far as your work is concerned, you are doing your country a favor by continuing to strive for success. The fewer people out of work and the fewer people asking for a handout, the better. You'll be particularly helpful to the overall economy if you take the chance on becoming a business owner. Employing other Americans is a patriotic endeavor, even if the government punishes you for doing it.

CHAPTER 11

YOUR ROLE IN POLITICS

You may have learned how a bill becomes law (at least the way it's supposed to become law), but very few young people are directly involved in politics. Some are simply disinterested, but others are unsure of how to get involved and what their roles might be. President Obama, for all his socialist legislation, was fantastic at getting young people involved in his campaign at the volunteer level. And that's a good place to start fighting against legislation like his.

First, Pick a Candidate

When you view the political landscape, it may seem as though none of the "viable" candidates is saying anything that directly appeals to you. And while that may be the case on the national or even state levels, the chances are you can find a local politician that is trying to accomplish something you'll appreciate. Even if the candidate is running for city council or the town's mayoral seat. Find a candidate like this to get behind; the experience might show you that real good can come from those elected.

Local politics is a great place to find a candidate because the issues being discussed in each election are likely to affect you and your family directly. Whether it's local taxes or school budgets, the local government has a huge impact on how your family lives. Maybe you care about the environment and want to see more done for local streams and ponds. While the environmental agencies at the state and federal levels have a say in how local municipalities handle their natural resources, the local government plays a major part in enforcing rules and regulations.

The point is this: all politics is local. Even presidential candidates have to show up to towns and cities across the nation to glad-hand the politicians and unions there. If you want the people representing you to be any random guy or gal that was able to muster up a few votes, then by all means continue ignoring local politics. But if you truly want to see change in your town or in your city, then by all means get involved and support a candidate that makes sense for you even if they don't have a chance at winning.

Vote

We talk in this book about earning the right to vote and how citizens shouldn't automatically be given the privilege of voting. That it should be earned. A society where 48 percent of the people don't pay federal **income** taxes is unsustainable. Not only do these people not pay income taxes, but they will also actually vote to raise income taxes because they are the beneficiary of such taxes. It's a vicious cycle of the supposedly nice politicians making sure you don't pay taxes to keep you dependent on the federal government (via your vote), which, of course, keeps them in power.

The reason we emphasize it so much is that any segment of the population that doesn't vote is summarily ignored by most politicians. They simply don't care as much about someone who cannot affect their chances of getting reelected.

By voting, you stand up for your generation, for your family, and for your interests. You can have a voice in politics, and the more kids who encourage their friends to vote, the more the youth in this country will have a say in politics. Turning eighteen means you are old enough to fight and die for this country; shouldn't you have a say in when we go to war and what happens to your friends? Vote!

Volunteering

Political campaigns are first and foremost about money. It costs tens of millions of dollars to run for the Senate and hundreds of millions of dollars to run for president. This money mostly goes to paying consultants and for the extremely expensive political advertising that is a part of every campaign. Consequently, there is a need to people who will work for free. Volunteering for a candidate of your choice is a great way to get your foot in the door of the political machine and often an eye-opening experience for those who choose to volunteer.

Whether it's making phone calls or going door-to-door, volunteers play a crucial role in getting the message to the people. If you people strongly in a politician's platform, you can help him or her by being an open advocate for policies in his or her platform. Most voters don't take the time to examine the proposed policies of each candidate; if you are an informed volunteer, you can help show these people the benefits of electing your candidate.

It's easy to become cynical when looking at the way politicians act. Many of them are guilty of corruption or at least catering to their most powerful contributors. But don't be a cynic. If we are all cynics, we'll never push for change. We'll all believe that it's not worth the effort, that nothing will ever change.

The Supreme Court voted in early 2010 to allow unlimited political contributions by corporations. For a long time, corporations were limited in what they could give because it was thought they were buying undue influence. The court suggested that it was a limitation on the First Amendment rights of the corporations to limit their contributions. Some may see this as influence peddling, but that shouldn't scare you away from getting involved.

Writing Letters

Writing a letter may seem like such a quaint act. Who writes letters anymore? Maybe your grandma and one or two relatives, but certainly not anyone under the age of thirty, right? Well, the truth is that a text or e-mail just doesn't have the impact that a physical letter does. Politicians respond to whomever they see as being most involved, and when they receive a physical letter, it shows that you care enough to write something and send it through the mail.

Senior citizens are considered a powerful force in politics because they do write letters. They call their congressmen and they campaign through organizations such as AARP. They are a constant presence in the thinking of politicians in this country because they have shown they care enough to write and care enough to vote.

Chapter 12

The Real Green Revolution

The real crisis in this country is not health care. Health-care "reform" is an attempt by the government to take control of an extremely profitable system in order to redistribute wealth from the haves to the have-nots. Besides, with illegal immigrants streaming across our borders and clogging our emergency rooms, a national system would be prohibitively expensive. The government would never be able to pay for it. No, our real crisis is energy. In fact, you could say energy represents the first, second, third, and fourth most important problems our nation faces. It is that important!

Imagine the collapse of society as we know it. Imagine living life without the ability to turn a light on at night or to drive to school. Imagine having to use candles again. Imagine having to stay by the fire during the winter to stay warm. Imagine your food spoiling after just a few days because you had no refrigerator. And what would happen to our supermarkets and hospitals?

We spend dozens of lives and billions of dollars a month in fighting wars to keep our flow of oil secure. But no matter how much we fight and which nations we invade, the truth remains that the oil supply is finite. It will run out no matter what we do. So why wouldn't a smart government spend whatever money it takes to get us off oil forever? Why do our leaders insist on allowing our nation to continue a policy of sending billions and billions of dollars every day to terrorists? We are dependent on countries who hate us; does that make sense?

Al Gore was vice president for eight years. He attempted to run for president and failed and was criticized for being "robotic" when he ran for president in 1999/2000. Those closest to him said that he was charismatic and humorous in person and that he had failed to convey those characteristics to the public when running for president. And then came *An Inconvenient Truth*, his crowning moment in the public spotlight.

Al Gore won an Academy Award and a Nobel Peace Prize for his work in *An Inconvenient Truth*. (Not to mention, Al Gore stands to make hundreds of millions of dollars if Obama's plan to redistribute wealth, through Cap and Trade, bill gets passed). He became more popular than ever before. People were listening to him, and they still do. But what Al Gore failed to emphasize is that more pressing issue for us as a nation is our dependence on foreign sources of fuel and our lack of real action in moving toward domestic sources. Besides, the proof that global warming is man-made is still tenuous, with controversy surrounding several prominent researchers and their efforts to produce objective data.

Much has been made of our dependence on fuel from the Middle East. After all, we've spent billions of dollars and thousands of lives in two wars there. Of course, the war in Iraq has little to do with foreign threats from terrorism and everything to do with Iraq's generous reserves of oil. Afghanistan may be different (it is not a supplier of much oil), but the fact remains that our wars are often linked to this dependence. But not all our oil comes from the Middle East. In fact, our largest supplier of oil is Canada. Should we invade Canada? No.

What we should do is realize that our nation is being crippled financially and politically by a lack of solutions in for solving these problems. As the supply of oil diminishes, our ability as a nation to pay for our insatiable thirst for the stuff will bring us to our knees. Think about the summer of 2008, when gas prices were at $4 per gallon of regular fuel in most of the country. It was crippling, and it slowed our tourism and travel industries to a crawl. Thousands of business had to make cuts or increase prices in order to pay for their gas! Pizza delivery services were charging extra gas fees, and families stopped going on long vacations. Airlines were on the brink of collapse.

This scenario played out for several months, but the reality is that once oil runs low, it will become a permanent scenario. That is, unless we as a nation decide to spend our tax dollars on things that will actually help us and not on bank bailouts. We talked about the CARS program earlier in the book. This program saw as many as 690,000 new cars on the road. That meant that just as many cars were being junked and sold off for scrap.

If the billions spent on that program was spent on actual green solutions—renewable energy—our country would be much better off in the long run. And we'd be even better prepared if the government ramped up its tax cuts to companies that are developing green technologies.

Just think about the seven-hundred-plus billion dollars that went to institutions that don't really make *anything*. The banks that received TARP funds are responsible for losing trillions of dollars in wealth. They repackaged debt and sold it off for a profit. They don't manufacture or produce any tangible service. So why did they receive so much money?

There are American companies that are pushing the technology of renewable energy that could have used that money to pull our nation closer to a clean energy-independent future. But politicians are so worried about getting reelected right now that they forgo developments that could help our country ten and fifteen years down the road. And since most of the major innovations we need to put us at the front of the green revolution will take that long to develop, we may never see them in time. Besides, the government has a vested interest in the continued use of gas. The federal government charges just over 18¢ per gallon in taxes. Considering Americans used 137 billions of gasoline in 2008, the federal government was making roughly $25 billion from the stuff.

We have to look at our dependence on foreign energy as being like when we were all kids that depended on our parents for a ride. If we wanted to go somewhere, we had to ask for permission. If we wanted to go somewhere our parents didn't approve of, we had to find another way to get there. And when we got older and we wanted true independence, we had to buy our own cars.

Right now OPEC (Organization of Petroleum Exporting Countries) has a tremendous amount of power over us and over Europe. This organization includes nations such as Libya, Saudi Arabia, Iraq, and Iran. If they decide to raise prices, there is little we can do about it. We are the kid that depends on our parents for a ride. They dictate the terms. If we want independence, we're going to have to "buy our own car" so to speak. We are going to have to provide our own energy in the future.

Private individuals such as T. Boone Pickens have been pouring their own money into providing for a clean-energy future based on U.S.-produced products. He has been trying to build wind farms in Texas and Oklahoma but has been running up against barriers both financially and politically in his efforts. Why hasn't the government made helping people like this a priority?

While entrepreneurial leaders like Pickens are doing their part to push us toward energy independence, they cannot marshal the resources we need to truly accelerate the pace of green-technology development. But the government can if it stops giving away trillions of dollars to collapsed banks and useless wars. One of the greatest threats to the American people is our dependence on foreign oil. We need oil more than almost any nation on earth does, and unfortunately it comes from people who don't exactly like us. In fact, it comes from countries that actively support terrorists trying to kill Americans.

The billions and billions of dollars used in the bailout should have been directed at overcoming this major obstacle to national freedom. If President Obama really wants to get the government involved in job creation, he should initiate a Manhattan Project-like effort to come up with viable energy sources that can liberate us from foreign suppliers. The Manhattan Project developed the nuclear bomb for the United States in the early 1940s, and no expense was spared to ensure its success. The brightest minds were put on the project, and work was done around-the-clock.

Everyone knows that our wars in Iraq have been about securing the oil supply our country desperately needs. We've lost thousands of soldiers because we need the precious oil the Middle East has, and we can't stand the thought of allowing the oil to fall into the wrong hands. We can avoid messy mistakes like the Iraq War if we use our technological might for the establishment of viable energy sources that are non-fossil-fuel-based.

Our country was able to put a man on the moon just sixty-three years after the Wright brothers first flew an airplane. We were able to create atomic weapons in the span of just a few years. We did these things by putting our greatest thinkers together and then supporting their efforts in an all-out push for success. When our nation decides to do something and really throws its resources at it, you can be assured it will get done.

As a young student, you have the ability to help in pushing forward the advancements in energy. One of the greatest services you can provide to your nation will be to help us get away from the billions and billions of dollars in payments we make to foreign oil producers. Most nations that we purchase from—Canada, Brazil, Mexico—are friendly to us. But there are nations, such as Iraq and Columbia, which offer us nothing but trouble. These nations don't deserve our money.

The future scientists and engineers of our nation are the ones that will determine whether or not we stay tethered to these nations. If these young people decide to dedicate themselves to renewable energies that can be produced domestically or in nations outside of OPEC, they will have helped us all.

It is key though that these pioneers receive the help they need from the government. Our wasteful wars in Iraq and Afghanistan are costing us dearly. In fact, gasoline was used as a benchmark in deciding the costs during a recent study. It turns out it costs us $800,000 a gallon to get the fuel to our troops because of the shipping, the security, the losses, and the remote regions in which we are operating. The capitalist society which America has always been encourages innovation like no other society in the history of the earth. It is this innovation and entrepreneurship that this country needs to encourage and not discourage.

Imagine if energy became so scarce it had to be rationed in the United States. In other words, envision a time that the government decides that your are using too much energy in your dorm room by using a TV, a stereo, and a computer that it could remotely, from an office in Washington, turn off your power. That sounds like a scary far off scenario but in fact the government has already purchased the technology to do just that. So much for living in a free country. Big government now has the ability to turn off your power.

The Future of the Global Economy

By the time you graduate college, the economy will be drastically different from how it was just ten years before. The free spending and booming markets will be gone, and in their places will be an economy that not only seeks growth, but also seeks a new kind of expansion. The new expansion will be into businesses, structures, and manufacturing techniques that are sustainable and clean. And the amount of work to be done is remarkable.

There are going to be trillions of dollars to be made in the green sector in the coming years. The nation that throws itself wholly into embracing these new technologies will be guaranteed a healthy, growing economy. India and China have unsurprisingly done just that. While these nations have yet to embrace stringent emissions standards for manufacturing or automobiles, they have made green technology a targeted area of expertise. They believe that by getting out front of the revolution, they can become the world's leader in manufacturing for solar and wind technologies, along with thermoelectric and natural gas.

In the United States, we have natural-gas reserves. We also have plenty of room in states such as New Mexico, Oklahoma, Texas, and Nevada for wind farms and solar plantations. We have the space, the know-how, and the incentive to make projects like these a priority. The only question is whether or not our government leaders are going to encourage growth in the alternative energy sector or if they will continue to throw away money on bailing out failing companies and irresponsible citizens.

So how does this relate to you? It will be the economy in which you try and find a job. Again, personal responsibility plays a part here. We've hammered home the importance of working hard in school and making sure that you have the skills you need to support your family. But what are those skills going to be, and how can you actually make sure you get ahead?

The first thing you can do is work hard. You'll be light-years ahead of many of your peers if you embrace the idea that working hard at a chosen career is something you should expect of yourself.

How You Can Help

Every one of us can help in the effort to create American innovations in the new green economy. If you're interested in science, you can work as an engineer or biologist and help our nation find new ways to free ourselves from oil. If you want to do something more immediate, you can encourage your friends and neighbors to recycle, carpool, use public transport, and take fewer trips for errands.

You can also encourage your local politicians to decrease government interference in the operations of American businesses that are developing green technologies. Tell them that you want our nation to be at the very forefront of the green revolution.

This entire book is about personal responsibility. It is about the idea that your own life and the choices you make are yours alone. You have the power to take care of yourself and to make a difference in your life and the lives of the people around you. If you want a green future, then start with yourself and then move outward to your family and friends. Don't just lament the fact that our country is burning too much oil. Find a way out for us and encourage your politicians to support it.

Let the people in power know that you aren't okay with bailout money and stimulus plans that support short-term political objectives. Tell them you want our nation's tax dollars to go toward long-term sustainability. Send an e-mail, or even better, a letter; and say how much you want to see wind farms and solar panels dotting the landscape. And tell your senator and congressman that on every single one of these structures you want to see "Made in the USA."

CHAPTER 13

SOLUTIONS

The federal government has long been looked at by young people as a great big monolith that cannot be changed or improved upon. They believe that no one within the system cares about the tax dollars, and they want to keep their jobs so they turn a blind eye to bureaucratic incompetence or even crimes. Right? Well, yes and no.

The government is made up of people, just like any other organization. Granted, government employees have some protections that the average worker doesn't enjoy like job security or the ability for their companies to print more money. But other than that, these employees make up each department and branch of the government. What's more important though is that each of these people ultimately works for their fellow citizens. They may not act as though they do, but in the end it will be your tax dollars and your votes that affect who is in charge of the government.

So what should you do to make sure that the policies and mistakes we've talked about so far are not continued? There are several things that can be done, and we'll look at each one in turn. These things include the following:

Securing Your Own Economy

The years following college can be difficult. You have student loans to pay off and a career to build. Meanwhile, some of your more ambitious friends have worked hard to get into good schools, they've majored in professions that pay well, and they're living a lifestyle you'd quite like to be a part of. You have decisions to make and tough ones at that.

Staying conservative and choosing to pay off your loans and save money can be gut-wrenching. You're young, you want to have fun, and who cares about tomorrow? Americans, and especially American youth, don't have a great track record of saving money. We're a live-for-today kind of nation, and that shows in the spectacular blowups which have racked our economy.

For just a moment though, think about your parents and their friends. How many of them will be able to retire when they hit sixty-five years old? How many are going to be depending on social security for their income? Do you know how much social security pays you? Not a lot.

Tomorrow, and specifically years from now, seems like a time that will never come. You worry about today and the things you want. Resisting the urge to buy toys now is very, very hard. That's understandable. But you can save. You can set aside a small amount to come out of your paycheck before you even see it. That little amount will make a difference for you one day, and you'll thank yourself for it.

Making It Better

George Washington thought the two-party system would never work because you either have to be loyal to your party or to the country. He may have been right. So many of today's political discourse is ruined by one party simply saying no to what the other party wants. And if one party really wants to get something done, they have to give away billions to opposition party members in order to buy their vote. It happens all the time, and it's about time it and all other wasteful spending by the government stopped.

By being an active citizen—writing to your politicians, working hard, and pushing for change—you can help to break the cycle of overfed politicians and their tagalong constituents. You can be the kid that confronts your project team member about their lack of effort. You can shame them into doing something different. You can make that kid (who will probably become a politician) pitch in and help in the project's completion.

If you and the hardworking kids like you push for enough change, from your peers and your politicians, the United States can turn back the clock. We can institute changes into the welfare, Medicare, and Medicaid systems that ensure the truly needy are helped. And that the truly lazy are forced to pitch in.

Your government is broken. But it is also fluid. You have the ability to help change it for the better, and the sooner you realize that your actions today are linked indelibly to your life tomorrow, the better off we'll all be. I know it seems that a system as large as the government is beyond your reach, but if there is one positive you can take from the Obama campaign, it's that grassroots efforts can become huge movements. The only difference is that the movement you start will be about real change: a return to a smaller, more efficient government that provides only what its people cannot and nothing more. Not fundamentally transforming America (from capitalism to socialism and communism) but **transforming America back to its fundamentals** of small government, liberty, and opportunity for all.

Pressure

Our country was never meant to have universal health care or large government bailouts or massive social programs. Our country is supposed to be about self-sufficiency and the rights and responsibilities of the individual. Our country is supposed to be an open marketplace with regulations in place only to protect the consumers. But we're becoming a country that is increasingly leaning toward the socialist structures that have plagued Europe for years.

Barack Obama's administration has put into motion efforts for further regulation (and in some cases outright ownership) of American companies and industries. His efforts are aimed squarely at taking away the responsibilities and benefits of private institutions to seek profits on their own and to collapse on their own. The bailout payments made by the government during 2009 were a travesty. They should have never happened.

When private institutions have failed in the past in this country the government has, for the most part, stayed out of it. And that's exactly what they should have been doing. If our economy is truly going to a free market, then businesses (even big banks) have to be free to collapse. Yes, other people will be hurt by these collapses and that includes innocent people, but that's the way our economy works. Businesses learn from their mistakes and will not repeat them. And this will eventually make their company stronger. The benefit of being able to build something from nothing is counterweighted by the realization that if you fail, you're on your own.

You can and should pressure your representatives to stand for free markets and small government. Make sure that when you vote, you're reading the actual platform of the politicians you're considering voting for. Don't be fooled by empty promises, and don't stop being involved as soon as you've pulled the lever to vote for someone. Being a good citizen means being active on a regular basis. Politicians don't like getting angry letters, and they especially don't like getting letters from thousands of their constituents. Making yourself heard and getting your friends involved can make a huge difference in how the country is run.

Politicians want nothing more than to be reelected. If their constituents make it clear that big government and socialist programs are not going to go down well with the voters in their districts, they'll vote against these programs.

The same goes for health care. Universal health care is a nightmare waiting to happen. If a physician is working for little pay and dealing with the bureaucracy of the government on a daily basis, how motivated will he or she be to get better at their work and to make sure everyone has been seen? Not very.

The best and the brightest become physicians because they want to help people and because they know that they can make a very good living at it. Making a profit is part of the equation, and if you take that away from physicians, you'll end up with less-than-stellar doctors.

An example of how horribly inefficient government regulation, consider the Cash for Clunkers program that was run in 2009. The program allowed thousands of people to get a $4,500 credit toward the purchase of a new car (what the government failed to mention was that each person who participated in the program would be taxed on the credit). It sounded like a good idea, and the government allotted roughly $1 billion for it up front. Unfortunately, that much money wasn't nearly enough. As usual, the government had wildly underestimated the cost of their socialist programs, and an additional $2 billion had to be written into new legislation to cover the ever-expanding program. So what do you think will happen if they take over health care?

The health care costs to Americans are too expensive, and reform does need to take place. But having the government run anything is a recipe for disaster, especially something as complex and critical as people medical care. Just look at Medicare and Medicaid. These programs are notorious for waste. Some people have estimated that these programs lose billions of dollars a year to fraud and inefficiency.

It's worth repeating here; the more taxes you levy on people (to pay for health care, etc.), the more jobs are lost. Employers will try to maintain their income by laying off workers every time taxes increase. Taxes kill jobs, plain and simple. With more people losing their jobs, more people will be dependent on the government. This is bad for you but good for politicians who cater to these "poor" people whose jobs were just lost, thanks to the politicians' own actions.

Budget for Yourself

Changing spending habits starts with individual Americans. If we as a people can change the way we view our personal finances, we can begin to understand just how wasteful our government has been. Imagine the following scenario: You earn $1,000 at your part-time job and use your parent's credit card to purchase $3,000 of shoes, some for yourself and some for your friends. Now you can imagine that your parents are going to have something to say about the situation and probably something you can't say on television.

But the reality is that people do this kind of thing all the time. The average American household has about $8,400 in credit card debt, whether they currently have credit cards or not, according to an April 2009 *Nilson Report* finding. Here's why that amount is so dangerous: First, even if you paid $150 per month and there were no interest on the credit card (wouldn't that be nice?) it would take more than four and a half years to pay the balance. Second, with the interest rates on today's credit cards (anywhere up to 30 percent interest in some cases), the $8,400 doesn't stay static. The amount owed on this balance will continue to climb until it is eventually paid off.

In total, Americans owe more than $1 trillion in credit card debt. That number is simply staggering, and it reveals a real problem of American culture: we spend as though there is no tomorrow. Until we as Americans learn to control our own spending, it will be difficult to convince politicians to be fiscally responsible. And if they aren't fiscally responsible, you can bet that the amount of money they borrow will be a lot more than $8,400.

There a thousand different schemes being peddled every day on the radio, on television, and in Internet ads, promising to help Americans reduce their debt payments. The reality is that most of them simply delay payments for years in order to reduce the monthly debt. That doesn't solve the problem; it simply delays the inevitable.

Personal sacrifice is an uncomfortable idea for most Americans. We want to find quick ways to solve our problems and we want those ways to be as pain free as possible. When it comes to paying off personal debt, there simply is no painless way to do it. Personal responsibility means doing what's right, regardless of the sacrifice. For most American families, paying of credit card debt would mean abandoning many of the spending habits we all take for granted: eating out, ordering in, buying things we can't pay for in cash, impulse buys, homes we can't afford, etc.

Ridding ourselves of debt means spending less than we make. It means creating a budget and cutting out any purchase that isn't absolutely necessary.

What if your parents took away your cell phone? What if they sold the TV and cancelled their Internet service? I imagine you wouldn't be too thrilled. Sacrifices like these are what most families would have to commit to in order to pay down debt. The reality is that most families will not embrace this mode of thinking. Most heads of household (the primary earner in each house) will carry debt forever.

Getting Students Out of Debt

According to Sallie Mae, 76 percent of undergraduate students had credit cards as of 2008. Half of all undergraduates at the time had four or more credit cards! And the average undergraduate had $2,200 in credit card debt when Sallie Mae collected their data. These numbers are shocking because they indicate that the average undergraduate has very little understanding of how credit works and what it means to carry a balance on a credit card. If you refer to the lesson on debt in this book, you'll see that carrying a balance (paying less than the total amount owed each month) results in interest payments that can dwarf the original amount borrowed on the credit card.

When these students go out into the world, they'll be arriving at their careers (or parents' house, depending on the job market and their skills sets) with debt upon debt because many students already have student loans which they'll be paying off for ten years or more. Add to that their growing credit card obligation, and you have someone headed for a life of monthly payments.

Why is it so important to avoid debt at your age? Because debt is a vacuum for money. The interest you pay on debt is "waste" money. It doesn't have anything to do with the price of the item you purchased. In other words, it isn't going toward "paying" anything except profit for the banks. There is a term in finance that explains principle: buying money. In order to borrow money from someone, you have to pay them for the privilege. But that's all the money is doing: paying someone for their services. It doesn't benefit you in the least unless you borrowed the money for investments and not for purchases.

In essence, people who take on debt are buying things twice. And that is where our national mentality needs to change. If you pay for something in cash, you pay for it once. That's a lesson we as Americans need to learn, and it's a lesson that needs to be pounded into the heads of everyone in Washington, D.C.

Government departments are given a fixed budget each year. The money they are allocated is part of the annual budget and is not turned over and used the next year if some is left over. The quest for funding for each department has to start anew and this of course presents a problem.

If you were in charge of a school program to buy books, and you were given $2,000 and told you had to spend all of it, you'd probably find a way to spend all of it. But what if your books only cost half of what you were given to spend? What do you do with the rest? You see, it's this kind of situation exactly that pushes government waste forward.

Each department knows that the money it is allotted each year is based in part on the money it spent the year before. If each department were to become as efficient as possible and to eliminate wasteful spending, they would soon find themselves with a small budget, something no department head wants. And the remaining money would in no way be returned to the taxpayers; instead, it would be funneled to other departments. So why not spend what you're given?

This, of course, creates all kinds of wasteful spending and unethical uses of taxpayer dollars. You can imagine what happens when department heads realize the end of the fiscal year is coming up and they have money they have to spend. Think about that the next time you pay your hard-earned tax dollars.

No More Bailouts!

Most people just don't understand how damaging many of President Obama's legislative initiatives will be in the long run. We hear the term "bailout" and we think of money to help banks and other financial institutions. The money also went toward buying up a major share in GM, and it went toward tax breaks for many Americans in the form of home-buyer's credits. But what does "bailout" really mean?

Here's an example using your irresponsible Uncle Sal. You see, Sal is a bit of a risk taker. He likes to start new companies, convinced that each one is going to make it big and that if he could just find the right idea, he'd be a billionaire. One day, Uncle Sal hits it big. He's making money hand over fist selling swampland in Florida. It's going so well that he borrows thousands of dollars from your parents to buy up more land. And then it happens: the swampland all floods and he loses his investment.

In a truly free market, your poor Uncle Sal would be out of luck, and so would your parents. Both Sal and your parents invested in an idea that was extremely risky. Swampland is prone to flooding, and Sal simply didn't have the money in reserve to weather a big downturn. And now he's broke and so are your parents, who invested their retirement fund in Sal's scheme.

But wait! The government has decided to help the real estate market recover and is looking for candidates who could use a bailout. Sal convinces the government that if he's bailed out, he won't ever engage in risky behavior again. The government is convinced and gives Sal $90,000 to get him back on his feet. Sal immediately flies to Italy for a three-week vacation. When your parents finally track him down, he refuses to pay them back; after all, investing is risky business, and you aren't guaranteed a return.

He likes to try new things and he likes to the government already has an ownership stake in the largest automaker in the country. And because the government is run by Democrats, the company was split up in bankruptcy court in a way that favored the union over bondholders, the people who had lent the company money. It was an outrage, but it was just the tip of the iceberg.

President Obama now has "ownership" in several large banks, automakers, mortgage companies, and more. What's more, the government just took over all student loans. That may sound good to people who are afraid of "evil" banks, but in reality it's not. The government will determine who gets loans and what schools they will grant more loans to. And we all know that the government is inefficient and political. Do we really want them deciding who goes to college and who doesn't?

The government should not be running private industries because no one can compete with the bankroll the government has. How are the competitors of these institutions supposed to compete with them when the government has their back and won't let them fail?

Give 'Em a Break

It's unfortunate that when the country is in need of more money, it automatically turns to businesses and the wealthy. The fact is that not all business owners are rolling in dough. And even if they are, it's because they took a chance and invested in the economy of the country. They worked hard, built a business, paid ridiculous taxes for payroll and income, and have earned their money.

Americans are sometimes hypocritical when it comes to their views of the wealthy. Many Americans despise the rich one minute and buy a lottery ticket the next. You see, everybody likes money; it's just that some people can't stand the sight of other people having it when they themselves don't. But if you look at job creation, you'll find that private industry is the place to do it, not through the government.

Government jobs programs do little to create long-term job growth. Once the allotted monies run out, the program is ended and the economy still hasn't grown strong enough to support the created jobs. It's only when private companies expand and hire more workers that real jobs are created. That is why more tax breaks should be given to business owners.

Business owners are the real drivers of the economy. They not only employ people, but they also put money back into the economy by buying supplies and products from wholesalers. Each business needs supplies in order to manufacture or market a product. Businesses want more customers, and when they want more customers, they advertise. Those advertising dollars are spread around the economy as much as the money spent on buying supplies is. It's a revolving system that spreads dollars around.

If you've ever thought about what you want for yourself long-term, consider business ownership. The wealth gap in this country has gotten larger but not because the wealthy are hoarding their money. It's because making good money in our economy means offering something that others can't or won't offer. That can be a cheaper product or a specialized skill.

Instead of giving the bailout dollars to the banks and businesses who failed, why not reward businesses that have survived or that are pushing technology forward? Why not use the bailout money for creating a new and better economy?

Starting a new business takes guts. It takes a willingness to risk your own personal money on a venture that has a high probability of failing. This failure could mean ruined credit, a loss of financial security in general, and even embarrassment or shame for the failed business owner. And yet Americans by the millions start new businesses every year. They do it because they believe what people have believed about America for centuries: that if you put in the effort and invest in the world's strongest economy, you can share in its copious rewards. You too can be a part of the most dynamic, most powerful economy the world has ever seen.

Why aren't these business owners being rewarded for taking this risk on our economy? In fact, why is it that the most successful of these business owners—and I'm not talking about just the billionaires here; any business that becomes profitable is a success—are being most severely punished? Imagine that you are a stellar student. You get straight As and work your butt off in order to move to the top of your class. You achieve the success your parents have wanted for you, and you've made yourself proud for being disciplined enough to make it happen.

After receiving your latest report card, you admire the line of As running down it and you swell with pride. You are approached by the assistant principal of your school and told that you have done very well. Congratulations on your work and thank you so much for making the rest of the school look good. You are a model student and your efforts are to be commended. And then you are informed that you have to give up part of your good report card to a "less fortunate" student.

It's a shame too. You work hard and you strive to succeed, and once you do, someone comes along and says that you have to give up far more of what you've earned than your less-successful neighbors will have to. Now some people will look at successful business owners, especially the very successful ones, and say "I don't feel sorry for them, they've got enough to give away." Yes, they do have enough to give away. And so would you if you worked an extra job or spend ninety hours a week building a business.

But if you worked long hours after going to school and doing your homework, you'd be more successful monetarily than your fellow students are. Would it be fair in this instance then to take half of what you've earned but none of what your fellow students are given by their parents as an allowance? No, it wouldn't be.

What our country should institute is a system of taxation that actually rewards those who put in the effort of bolstering the economy. What's wrong with a flat tax, for example? Why should the wealthy lose more of what they've earned? Our nation is supposed to offer equal protections under the law for all citizens. So why are people who earn more money singled out for different treatment? They don't get anything extra from the government for the money they put into the system. It's not like the government shows up to their homes a few times a month with a menu and asks them if they would like their roads repaved or perhaps a surplus tank they might have paid for at one point.

Everything in our society, up until the point we come under the watchful eye of the federal government (usually eighteen years of age), encourages us to excel. In elementary school, we are given gold stars and certificates for getting good grades. In middle school, we are put on the honor roll, and in high school we are designated as valedictorian or honor student when we do well. And then we get into the "real world" of careers and businesses; and all of a sudden, those who excel are told that instead of a reward, they will be required to sacrifice more than those who have not done as well.

Imagine if you will our country with a flat tax. Everyone pays 15 percent of their income. The wealthy would still be paying far more in a monetary sense than the average person would, and yet they would be able to keep a greater percentage of what they earned. That would be money they could give to charity, spend on their businesses, use to buy products and services thereby providing jobs, and so on. It has been proven time and again that lowering the tax burden on high earners stimulates spending and job creation.

What if you had $500 in your pocket and had to cut your parents' lawn on Saturday? However, your friends asked you to play basketball that day. Just then, a kid without $500 knocks on your door, asking to cut your lawn for $20. You would probably give him the $20 because it's a good deal for you and now you can go to your basketball game. Congratulations, you have just created a job. The best way to create jobs in this country is to lower the tax burden on everybody. The only way to do this is to shrink the size of the federal government.

Securing the Borders

So how do you fix the problem of border security? Well, the issue of border security is a little bit outside the scope of this book, and I don't expect you do go out and do battle with the drug cartels. So for this section we'll focus on illegal immigration. The fixes for this problem are similar to those for fixing other problems in that you focus on eliminating demand and the rest of the issue will be easier to deal with. Terrorism, of course, is a different matter, but this book isn't about intelligence gathering so much as it's about making America better in an everyday sense.

So how do we solve illegal immigration? After all, you can't secure two thousand miles of border completely, and you can't build enough prisons to house all of the illegals already in the country. And you can't deport twelve million people all at once. The fix is actually four-pronged: financial penalties, social resistance, legislative reform, and law enforcement.

So what if we amended the Fourteenth Amendment? What if we changed it so that people born within this country are only citizens if their parents are in the country legally? What would that do to the incentives some people see in coming here? What if they knew that their children could legally be deported back to their home countries? Would so many come here?

And what if we made hiring an illegal alien a felony? What if employers knew they would face five years in prison for hiring an illegal alien? The results, I assure you, would be stunning: if fewer employers hire illegals, not only they would be forced to hire American citizens (of all backgrounds), and that would help to fuel our economy. It would be win-win for Americans.

Granted, some of our products and services would get more expensive because American workers demand better treatment and better wages. But our businesses would adapt, and we'd all be better off for it. Besides, if a company is staffed by illegal immigrants and their work turns out to be shoddy, do you think that company is going to be stand-up about it and refund you your money? Do you think a company that hires illegals without really caring about their backgrounds is also going to be part of the Better Business Bureau? Probably not.

So many things would improve if we took away the rewards for crossing our borders illegally. Our health-care system would spend fewer dollars treating the uninsured; our businesses could charge fair prices for good work. We could know that the children in our schools are there legally and that our resources are not being wasted on people who haven't obtained citizenship legally.

In fact, many school systems have residency investigators on the payrolls. In order to get their children into the best school system possible, families will have their children live in different towns than they do, often with a distant relative or a friend. Or they'll simply use this friend's or relative's address and drive their children into town each day. Of course this means that school districts have to supply instruction and supplies for children who aren't residents. This stretches budgets and makes capacity planning difficult for many school districts that are surprised by the number of students registering for schools, more students than are projected to actually live in the town.

Most people don't know about these investigators. And in fact, in most countries, these students and their parents would be summarily dismissed from the country. But not here. Here, we simply tell them they can't attend the school they've been fraudulently using as their personal "private" education. Everybody understands wanting to better your situation, but when you do it illegally, you should be treated as a criminal.

Border security is not being enforced, and that leaves our nation weak on many levels. There are not just well-meaning workers crossing the border illegally. Drugs, prostitutes, and other human slaves are coming across the border in droves. It's a danger to the public and a symptom of lax security. Along with these, more common criminals could come worse, perhaps terrorists.

As a young person, you have the opportunity to make a real difference in this realm. We all want our nation to be a welcoming and receptive place for legal immigrants looking to make a better life. By allowing illegals to enter the country and to use up jobs and resources, we make life harder for those trying to come here legally.

People attempting to come to this nation legally are often lumped in with those that have sneaked across the border. They are treated as though they don't have a right to be here because they look like, or speak the same language as, people who are making the news for sneaking in by the millions.

Securing the borders is not an easy task. It's virtually impossible to watch several thousand miles of border 24/7. But the more people we allow to use up precious federal and state resources, the harder we make it for people who are genuinely in need of support.

As you move on from school, you'll realize that making a decent living is hard enough and that competing with another businessman or businesswoman who employs cheap illegal labor is impossible. Our economy is punishing qualified workers by allowing illegals to drive down the cost of labor.

If you happen to go into one of the skilled crafts, chances are you'll be competing against people who will work for half of what you're qualified to charge. Perhaps your parents are already running into this problem. If you're father is a carpenter or a carpet layer, he's probably making less than he might if our nation was stricter with border security.

Financial Penalties

Because it's likely that most illegal immigrants are going to stay in the country, their citizenship and position in society cannot be simply handed over. They have lived here illegally and have avoided paying taxes. Their "amnesty," if you want to call it that, should be contingent on paying back taxes and in submitting themselves to citizenship exams just as difficult as those taken by legal immigrants.

Social Resistance

Illegal immigrants can thrive in this country because our society bends over backward to bring them into the fold. Whether it's businesses offering services in Spanish, schools offering classes in Spanish, or American citizens putting up with their service providers hiring illegal immigrants, we have gone too far as a people in accommodating people who are not a part of our society legally. Imagine if every home owner refused to hire contractors who had illegal immigrants on their payrolls. Imagine if schools stopped allowing the children of illegal immigrants to attend schools. What if businesses stopped offering services in Spanish when you called their hotlines?

The point is that if this country weren't as welcoming to illegal immigrants as far as employment and living arrangements, then they wouldn't be coming here with such regularity. This is not a call for angry mobs or for rudeness toward illegal immigrants, just an acknowledgment that we as a people are partly responsible for allowing illegals to live so easily in our country.

Legislative Reform

Democrats love illegal immigrants. They love them because they know if they accommodate them then their children will be lifelong Democrats. They don't mind harming the country in exchange for a permanent seat at the table.

And if illegal immigration continues unabated, our population will soon reflect the desire of Democrats to do get exactly that. We predict that during the Obama administration there will be a big push to legalize all illegal aliens. Not for the good of the country, or to be fair, but to secure votes and stay in power. So what can be done legislatively (provided the right people are in office)?

The first thing is for Americans to start making illegal immigration a priority issue when voting. If politicians want to get elected, they must satisfy the desires of their constituents. It's not a secret that politicians pander. But if real pressure were put onto sitting politicians or those running for office, then real change could take place. So what would, should, the voters force these politicians to do?

Why do illegal immigrants risk jail and death trying to cross the borders of our country, be it from the Caribbean, Mexico, Latin America and South America, Europe, or Canada? Jobs. Employment on a grand scale. Employers hire illegal immigrants by the millions. Sometimes so many illegals are working for the same plant or factory that they take over entire towns by virtue of their numbers. The towns are forced to accommodate a population that isn't even legally in the country.

Employers carry a massive amount of the blame in the fight over illegal immigration. In an effort to save money, employers look for cheaper labor. They find it in illegals for whom they have to provide no benefits and little pay. They don't have to claim them on their taxes and they don't have to worry about them claiming worker's compensation or complaining about miserable working conditions. In essence, these employers have voluntary indentured servants.

When one employer in a particular field hires illegals and slashes prices, his or her competitors are forced to do the same. After all, they can't compete against someone offering the same work for half the price. And if they try and do the right thing and hire only legal residents, they will quickly find themselves priced out of the market.

It is up to legislators to make hiring illegal immigrants not worth the consequences. If an employer knows that raids on businesses employing illegals are common and that the punishments are severe, they'll have to think long and hard about whether or not it's worth it. What if each employer faced time in jail? What if they knew that getting caught meant a year in jail for each illegal they employed? Do you think they would hire more illegals?

By starting at the source of the problem, legislators can take away the incentives for illegal immigrants to make the journey here in the first place. It will take a lot of political will to make this happen, but the cost of not doing so is tremendous to us as a nation.

Law Enforcement

As it is, law enforcement officials are overwhelmed by the number of illegal immigrants making their way into the country. Budgets are stretched thin, and many local law enforcement officers have little recourse when they find out someone living in their town is in the country illegally. Federal authorities are so busy with mass raids and arrests that one illegal guilty of driving drunk or of jaywalking is not worth their trouble. That leaves a major gap.

These agencies need greater powers to go after the employers that are hiring illegal aliens. For example: When day laborers are looking for work, they gather in the parking lots of home-improvement stores and along regularly traveled thoroughfares. They know that the contractors will come to them if they need cheap labor for the day. So why aren't they being arrested if they're gathering in open daylight? Again, it comes back to the constitutional issue of illegal search and seizure. An officer can't go around asking people for identification if they aren't committing a crime.

With reasonable suspicion though, these officers ought be allowed to ask for identification. They ought to be allowed to go with what they know to be true: the men waiting outside the hardware store are not here legally. They shouldn't be allowed to buck the system that openly without any fear of retribution.

Giving to Those in Need

Currently, cities and states require most welfare recipients to hold jobs, and many recipients do work diligently to get off welfare. Being down and out is not easy. It's a humiliating experience for most and something they want desperately to overcome. But because our social programs are run by the government, they are horribly inefficient and easy to scam.

There are people in this country unfortunately who still act as though they were the weak link in a group science project in high school. They don't put in the efforts to get off welfare; in fact, many of them prefer to be on welfare and do what they can to increase their weekly payments. This includes having more children so that they can get more checks. It's a horrible practice, and it costs Americans billions of dollars a year.

Making social programs more restrictive is a tricky business because you don't want to harm those Americans who have genuinely worked hard and have just fallen on hard times through a company closure or bank failure. These men and women deserve some assistance. Helping them and excluding others can be accomplished in several ways.

First, closer monitoring of employment status is a must. We have to make sure that Americans receiving assistance are actively looking for work and that if they say they're employed, they actually are.

Second, we need to eliminate certain privileges citizens enjoy if certain people are unwilling to contribute to the economy. One way to do this would be to revoke the right to vote for people who haven't paid federal income tax in two years or more. This may seem cruel, given that many people are unable to work or are stay-at-home moms, but these people wouldn't be affected by this law. As long as someone in the home is earning an income and actively contributing to the economy, the members of the household will be able to vote. Retirees would also be excluded from this law.

Third, the government must come down harder on people who try and game the system. It is unacceptable that so many people are able to defraud the system with little fear of real retribution. Can you imagine being in a school where detention lasts just five minutes and those kids who cheat are simply told not to do it again? It would be lawless, and that is what so many of our social programs have become.

If our nation dedicates itself to weeding out those who want nothing more than to float by on someone else's dime, we'll be able to save billions of dollars that can be put toward education, energy research, and most importantly, paying off the deficit.

The War on the Deficit

Then I say the earth belongs to each of these generations during it's course, fully, and in their own right. The 2d. generation receives it clear of the debts and incumbrances of the 1st., the 3d. of the 2d. and so on. For if the 1st. could charge it with a debt, then the earth would belong to the dead and not the living generation. Then no generation can contract debts greater than may be paid during the course of it's own existence."

Most people in our country can't imagine just how vast our national debt really is. It's reported to be over $12 trillion, but what does that mean to the average person? What it means is just over $39,000 per American. At least if you believe what you're being told by most authorities. The real number of unfunded liabilities for the United States government (including Medicare and social security) is about $110,000,000,000,000. That's $110 trillion.

This means that each one of the 309 million Americans owes over $350,000. The number is rising so fast that by the time you are reading this book, it's billions of dollars higher.

The number 110 trillion is so vast it's almost impossible to understand the implications. But just the interest accruing on the loan is enough to make your head explode. As mentioned above, the debt increases by more than $3 billion a day. That's enough money to make you one of Forbes's wealthiest Americans; and it's counting against our national debt every single day, seven days a week, all year long.

Taxing each American $350,000 all at once is obviously impossible, and so the deficit just keeps growing and growing and growing out of control. In fact, in 1791, shortly after the founding of our nation, the national debt was $75 million. That's a large sum, but still nothing compared to today's debt, even adjusted for inflation. In fact, our debt grows by that amount nearly every day. And it's a recent phenomenon. Our national debt didn't surpass $1 trillion until sometime around 1981, just a few years before most of you reading this book were born.

But since that time it has skyrocketed, with no signs of slowing down. Unfortunately, President Obama doesn't believe in reducing this debt any time soon. Sometimes Democrats are called the "tax and spend" party and for good reason. We owe a lot of people a lot of money and yet they're handing out dollars as though they were coupons at a supermarket.

Our national debt is a huge threat to our country. We simply cannot borrow money forever. We cannot continue down this path or the dollar will become worthless, we will lose our ability to borrow money, and our standing as a nation at the top of the pyramid will quickly evaporate. But this book is about personal responsibility more than anything, so why am I talking about the national debt so much?

There is perhaps no better lesson in personal responsibility than debt. Debt is an often misunderstood aspect of finance, and it's never really explained to kids your age. I mean how often do you take time in school to learn about balancing a budget, interest, credit cards, or even paychecks and taxes? I would wager never. And yet debt and credit will play a constant role in the rest of your life. Heck, it plays a role in your life now; you just don't know it. Your parents are likely in debt because they are paying off their house over time. They are likely paying for their cars over time as well and so must have borrowed money with interest attached.

The money your parents have borrowed, and how diligently they have paid it back, will play a part in how easily they can secure student loans for you should you decide to go to college. It will dictate the terms they can secure on any loans, such as time to pay back and the interest the lender will charge. The worse a person's credit (or history of repaying borrowed money) is, the bigger a risk it is to lend them money, and so lenders charge more for the service.

The same holds true for our country and the same will hold true for you. There is good debt and bad debt: good debt is used to borrow money for the creation of businesses or to buy homes; bad debt is money borrowed for items that will lose value and are not going to help you repay the debt. Many young college students fall into the trap of borrowing a lot of money at high interest rates and it takes them years to pay it off. If they fall behind on the payments, they ruin their credit, and it can take years more to restore it.

One of the greatest challenges most college kids face is that of credit cards. The credit card companies pay universities for the right to advertise their credit cards directly on campus and offer "free" handouts to students who sign up. The problem, of course, is that these credit cards have astronomical interest rates. And the students who sign up for them seem to have no clue that they will have to pay the money back plus interest. Well, invariably parents across the country get phone calls from their kids who desperately need money to pay of the swelling debts. If they can't pay them off, their credit is ruined, and so they have trouble borrowing money for things like home repairs.

The same cycle of overspending and borrowing is bringing the United States to its knees in a financial sense. Foreign nations are the ones lending us the money. They buy U.S. Treasury bonds by the truckload in exchange for repayment with interest. And that interest is precisely all we're paying. We haven't touched the principle. So what does this mean for your country in the long run? It means the same fate enjoyed by those college freshman and their parents: bad credit.

Eventually, the countries lending us money will realize we are in a position we are in over our heads. We will become a "bad bet" creditwise, and they will stop lending to us. Without this constant flow of income from lenders, our country will freeze up, and the economy will collapse. Our nation spends more than it makes. It has for years now, and the reality is that eventually the bill for all this overspending comes and we won't be able to pay the bill.

Overcoming this dilemma will take a dedication that reflects that which we've thrown into our wars. We must look at our deficit as an enemy and make a conscious decision to sacrifice in order to pay it down. That means cutting back, and that's never a popular decision. If your parents told you that your allowance was being cut in half, you'd probably disapprove of the decision. Well, cutting the deficit is going to mean having a president with the tenacity and courage to start cutting major programs, programs that congressmen and senators want to keep.

That same spirit of sacrifice is something you have to embrace as an individual citizen if you want to avoid the negative consequences that tremendous debt can bring. By avoiding bad debt and by smartly managing your money, you can keep yourself financially secure. You can stay away from the mistakes that have brought our economy to its knees.

But that begs the question: if debt of the magnitude is so bad, then why do our politicians insist on adding to it? Well, there are a couple of reasons for this, and they relate directly to the kind of spending that college freshmen do with their new credit cards. You see, the reason these politicians spend so freely is that they know it looks good to a certain segment of voters. They can go on TV and say "Look, we're spending money to stimulate the economy and give you your jobs back."

The reality, of course, is that they cannot guarantee these jobs back. They can only make empty promises. But those promises often work in getting them reelected. And they know that getting reelected is all that matters. Besides, they aren't the ones that have to repay the debt. They leave that to some future politician to figure out. For right now, they want to spend as much as necessary to improve their district or state so that they can keep their jobs. They'll say they want to pay down the debt or that they're trying to be fiscally conservative but they'll spend anyways. Just look at the Republican-controlled Congress prior to the Democrats taking control in 2006: they spent billions of dollars on bailouts and spending packages deceptively named as stimulus and jobs bills. All politicians will spend blindly; they'll just justify the spending in different ways. The Democrats will say it's for the social good, and the Republicans will say it's for the safety of the people.

Keep your finances in order so that you don't have to look to the government to be our baby daddy. They'll likely support you, but the cost to our nation will be more than you can calculate. Do you really want to be part of the problem?

Recap: Lessons Learned

Blessed is he who expects nothing, for he shall never be disappointed.

—Unknown

It's a saying that seems overly pessimistic, but in reality is a mantra that the young people of this country should adopt when thinking about their personal goals and ambitions. You should adopt that attitude that you will work for and support yourself and your family. That you will put in the time and effort it takes to get good grades, graduate college or a trade school, find decent work, and become a productive member of society.

I'm sure you've seen in school or among your friends which ones take responsibility for what they've done. The friends who don't ask for help unless they need it but are there to help others. These people draw others close to them by virtue of their character. They don't wait for someone else to fix their problems, they don't whine about life, and they don't try and get out of following through on their responsibilities. These people are admirable and becoming all too rare.

You can be one of these people. Think about how different your life will be from now on if you take the attitude that no one is going to give you anything. Imagine that from now on there is now welfare, there is no such thing as a government subsidy, and there is no such thing as bailouts or handouts or tax breaks for the poor. Imagine that our economy, though regulated, truly rewards the creative and the ambitious. Think about what that attitude of personal responsibility and action will do for you.

So many people in our society sit back and wish they had a good job or a nice house or a business of their own. They want someone to give them something; they want more help doing these things than they deserve. And you know what? The government is trying its best to give it to them . . . at the expense of the people who actually work every day.

Redistributing wealth, something that the Obama administration is heavily focused on, is a recipe for disaster. Trying to prop up the less fortunate by stealing from the more fortunate will do nothing but bring the entire country down. People who are making money will move it out of the country or fire more workers. As we know, the only way to prop up the less fortunate is to allow the more fortunate to provide jobs for them.

Protect and Serve, Nothing More

Your government's job is to protect your rights, both physical and constitutional. They are also responsible for providing services to the citizens of this country that each citizen cannot provide for him or herself. And they have a responsibility to deal with other nations on our behalf. They should not be involved in much more than that. The idea that the government should get involved in private industry to the point of ownership is downright socialism. Their involvement in massive corporate and personal handouts is even worse.

Clean Domestic Energy=Freedom

With all the talk about green energy and the efforts to halt global warming, many have overlooked just how perilous our situation is as a nation. We use a tremendous amount of fossil fuel every day, more than any other nation on earth does. In fact, we use more than twenty million barrels of oil per day! Per day! And we don't have all that oil here in our country.

To be truly independent of the blackmail oil-producing nations have perpetrated against us for years, we must make domestic, renewable energy our number one priority. It should be treated the way we treated the mission to the moon. We should be throwing billions of dollars a year at this problem because if we don't secure energy independence, we will be powerless when it comes to diplomatic negotiations, trade talks, or energy pricing on a global scale.

Term Limits

When congressmen and senators are lifelong members of the legislature, they essentially become wards of the state. Their careers become entirely focused on being a senator or congressman and they desperately want to cling to their positions. But in order to stay in one of these positions, you must raise millions of dollars a year in campaign funds. To do that, you need friends with millions of dollars in disposable income. These "people" or more likely corporations and interest groups, don't give donations out expecting nothing in return. They want their political and financial agendas supported, and for the most part, congressmen and senators toe the line for these people. Without the pressure of being reelected over and over, our politicians would free to serve the people.

Some of these politicians will say that to be effective as a senator they need time to "learn" and seniority in order to gain influence. But as has been proven time and time again, these senators and congressmen grow increasingly distant from the real problems of the people they are supposed to serve. Few have jobs outside of being a politician and few understand the world outside of Washington, D.C., after living and working there for twenty-plus years.

Political parties and unions have their own agendas and desire to stay powerful

If a union is not helping the company that employs its workers, then the union is detrimental to the process of creating products and services. In order for an organization to work at its best, there must be a common goal between the union and employers. There must be an agreement that while the worker's rights are important and the company's profits are important, neither will improve if the union and the company are working against each other.

Unfortunately, many organizations are now engaged in a sort of cold war with their unions. They search out ways to limit pay and benefits as the union looks for ways to increase both. Older, better-paid employees are targeted for removal because they earn too much money. The unions ensure that employees receive increases in pay whether or not their value to the company has increased.

The union doesn't care if an employee is making $71 an hour to perform a relatively simple task. If the employee is earning more, they're paying more in dues, and the union gets richer.

The government has already replaced the need for unions in areas of worker safety and wages. The government guarantees worker's rights through whistle-blower laws, minimum wage, overtime laws, OSHA, and more. Workers are more protected now than they have ever been. Now laws that protect the workers and unions are rapidly becoming obsolete and a drain on our money. In fact, the only union that is growing in size is the government workers union.

Rewarding the Brave

The people who built this nation were the dreamers, the big-thinkers, and the small businessmen and businesswomen who ventured out into the unknown and took a chance on our nation's economy. It was not build by union leaders or the government. While union members have obviously played a huge role in the workforce in our nation, their bosses have become more a hindrance to our country's economic well-being than a regulating force. They tie up work in order to eke out extra dollars for themselves and are often working against the best interests of the company their members work for.

If you've always heard that unions are a good thing and that without them our workers would simply be crushed under the industrial machine, that's probably because of where you get your information. Teachers are members of unions almost nationwide. If they're teaching you about unions, their views are likely to be slanted in favor of the work that unions perform. And while there is a great and respected history in our nation of unions breaking down barriers and securing certain guarantees for workers everywhere, they are no longer acting in the same capacity. Don't let your teachers, or anyone else, make you feel that you are not smart or academic because you see things in a different light. You have a right to question what it is unions are doing now, and the deeper you dig into their activities, the more you'll realize that they have become a problem more than a solution.

Safe at Home

What defines a nation more than its geographical borders? Yes, the people of a nation and its government play a role are defining "who" the nation is. But more than anything, nations are defined by their borders. And can any nation claim that it is keeping its citizens safe if it cannot secure its own borders? No, it cannot. The government primary job is the safety of its citizens. If it is not performing that basic task, the government is a failure. Shouldn't we feel safe in our own nation? It's bad enough that criminals make us feel unsafe in our homes; but to think that terrorists, drug smugglers, people smugglers, and other criminals can all simply walk across our borders is terrifying.

Why has this problem persisted? Why have politicians treated this simply as part of our economy or as a nuisance more than a real life-and-death problem?

Yes, our nation has poured billions of dollars into fighting the drug war; and yes, they have increased the number of border guards. But they have done little inside of the country to guarantee that illegal immigrants cannot find employment, cannot take advantage of our educational system, and cannot slip through the cracks in order to raise their children as Americans. We Americans are just as guilty because for years we have looked the other way and supported businesses that hire illegals. That has to stop.

Learn English, Be American

It may seem outrageous on the surface to ask America's citizens to stop calling themselves African American or Asian American or Caucasian even. But that's exactly what we need. You may be saying, "That's racist," or "Why shouldn't people be able to call themselves what they want?" I assure you; the reasoning behind this change is anything but divisive.

In any nation, there are subcultures, groups of people with common backgrounds and common cultural leanings that identify with one another. There is nothing wrong with that. America has been blessed to be home to a great number of fascinating influences from across the globe. The problem though is when members of each subculture see their individual cultural backgrounds as more important than they do the United States as a whole.

When we label ourselves as being Asian American or Latin American or African American, we take away a part of our common bond as a people. One of the most compelling ideas in American culture is the idea that "united, we stand," one nation. If we had viewed each other as equal partners in the American experiment over the years, we could have avoided many of the uglier chapters in our history.

During WWII, Americans of Japanese descent were rounded up and put into internment camps. These citizens were in many cases second—and third-generation Americans. They were born and raised here, and yet we treated them as outsiders. What if our government had looked at them simply as Americans? What if we viewed legalized immigrants as fully American, as part of our family? We could eliminate so many of our problems.

If you want to feel more united with your neighbors, your teachers, your friends, and your family, think of each of them as Americans first. Above all, respect your fellow Americans even if they weren't born in the United States. Do what you can to help them assimilate into our culture for the common good of the country. That doesn't mean asking them to forget everything about where they came from. You don't have to banish their wedding rituals or their decorations in their homes. But helping them to learn English, helping them to learn our customs and our social discourse, will be helping them to feel more at home here.

The Progressives in our government are determined to help everyone feel as comfortable as possible even if that means ignoring the roles that immigrants could play in our society if learning English and dropping these silly labels was compulsory. By overembracing their urge to "respect" everyone's culture, they are insulting the great benefits of being a part of the American culture. You would think that some liberals were ashamed of being American, as though the mistakes we've made in the past were enough to tarnish our image forever.

If people feel that heritage labels are important, we propose that one should say "I am an American of African descent or Asian descent," etc. This emphasizes that you should be an American first, and if this is not where your allegiance lies, then you should be living somewhere else.

Freedom in Giving

We are a giving people, the most giving on the planet. We give more money than any other nation by a good margin. Each year, Americans donate more than $260 billion to charitable organizations, including religious institutions. As a percentage of our gross domestic product, or GDP (GDP is an economic measure which approximates the worth of each economy), that's more than any country has.

What's interesting about this fact is that it's assumed Americans are greedy because we don't want socialized institutions in our nation. We don't want really high taxes weighing us down. You would think that socialized countries would give more because the people were more "generous," but that isn't the case. In fact, France, a very socialized country, is in the embarrassing position of having some very stingy residents. The French give around 0.15 percent of their GDP, with Americans giving 1.8 percent.

The problem with all this generosity is that it is being threatened by Barack Obama and other Democrats who feel that taxes are the best way to give back to the needy. But who you give your money to is an intensely personal decision.

If you have a relative battling cancer, you might give to cancer research. If you know someone whose child has autism, you might give to an organization searching for a cure to that dreaded condition.

The point is, you've earned your money, and you have the right to give it to whomever you want. But that right has been slowly taken away from us as American citizens. The government has decided that they will use our tax dollars as a large charity fund where everyone gets a piece. But they haven't just stopped with the tax dollars we've paid to them in the past. Barack Obama and his administration want to raise taxes on the upper-middle classes (the business owners in our country) so that he can give away even more money. He's everyone's rich uncle, but instead of a rich uncle who's earned his own money, Barack Obama is like Bernie Madoff. He's taken everyone else's money and is now dishing it out to whomever he feels should have money they didn't earn redistributed to them.

Why does our government not think that we as a people of capable of giving to charities we see fit for our contributions? This is an example of a government structure that thinks very little of its citizens. We can't be trusted to take care of our fellow citizens and we can't be trusted to contribute to the economy and so our government is laden with social programs designed to do it for us.

With ever-increasing taxes and a shrinking economy, fewer Americans are going to shell out money to charities. If budgeting comes down to paying the mortgage or giving to that local charity you've supported for years, the mortgage is going to win. With tax cuts, more Americans would be free to give to nonprofits. The benefit of this generosity would go well beyond the government programs that are currently threatening to suck up all of these dollars.

No Pay, No Play

Did you know that only 52 percent of all households pay federal income taxes? That's right; forty-eight percent of the millions of American households don't pay any income taxes to the federal government. But these people are still granted all the rights and privileges that tax-paying Americans enjoy. In fact, the government now says that we all have the right to health care. It should be known however that the government cannot grant nor take away rights. Any institution with the power to give has the power to take away.

I'm all for having some universal rights such as freedom of religion and the full use of the courts, but why should everyone have a say in the goings-on of our government? If you've never held a job or put in work and sweat into the economy, why should you be able to dictate our leadership? The people going to work every day and paying into the federal government should have the right to say who runs the country. They are the ones putting in the time and energy to keep our economy moving. There should, of course, be exceptions; for example, if you are a retiree and are not earning an income, you should still be able to vote. You've put in your time and deserve a say.

Voting had lost a lot of its luster in the country prior to the 2008 election when participation increased dramatically. There are many reasons for that, one of which being that changes in president or senator rarely result in dramatic changes in the everyday lives of Americans. That's a testament to how stable our country has been and also how little our politicians accomplish. But things have changed over the last couple of years, and now our country is in danger of becoming something it was never meant to be: socialist. Voting will grow more important as people realize what is happening, and it will once again be viewed as a privilege.

This privilege should be earned, not handed out. Voting and making your voice heard should be something we as Americans earn the right to do.

We hope you have learned some real truths by reading this book. In future books we will show you where our country is headed and what kind of people we have leading our country. Peaceful action is the only way we can save our country and bring it back to its fundamentals. It is now your personal responsibility to do something about it. Now you have learned a very important lesson—if the system is broken at the bottom (illegal immigrants, segmented subpopulations of Americans that do not assimilate into the American way of life, sense of entitlements even when all of our entitlement programs are bankrupt and bankrupting the country, huge government with inefficient and wasteful spending strapping hundreds of thousands of dollars onto the back of every American), you do not fix it by stealing money from those who have played by the rules and have achieved the American dream and penalizing those who create the jobs in this country. The president is doing precisely that—massive increase in borrowing, spending, and government growth and control; slapping huge tax increases on anyone who can pay, causing massive losses of jobs, devaluation of the dollar, and therefore creating more dependency on a bankrupt government. If you are still not convinced that big government with massive tax and spend policies and large entitlements will ruin this country, look across the Atlantic. Almost every socialist country is on the verge of disastrous bankruptcy and civil unrest. It is up to you to make sure that we do not head down the same deadly path.

You cannot help the poor by destroying the rich.
You cannot strengthen the weak by weakening the strong.
You cannot bring about prosperity by discouraging thrift.
You cannot lift the wage earner up by pulling the wage payer down.
You cannot further the brotherhood of man by inciting class hatred.
You cannot build character and courage by taking away people's initiative and independence.
You cannot help people permanently by doing for them,
what they could and should do for themselves.

—Reverend William John Henry Boetcker

Now, a **POP QUIZ!**

1. Fill in the blank: A _____ believes in fundamentally transforming America from a capitalist republic to communism one step at a time.
    a. Republican
    b. Progressive
    c. Libertarian
    d. Democrat

2. Redistribution of wealth as championed by President Obama
    a. Takes away incentive to be successful
    b. Creates class warfare
    c. Kills jobs
    d. All of the above

3. Which of the following racial designations would be best to describe Dr. Martin Luther King Jr.?
    a. American of African descent
    b. Black
    c. African American
    d. Colored

4. Which of the following truly stimulates economic growth?
    a. Government spending
    b. Increasing government debt via bailouts
    c. More government programs
    d. Tax reduction

5. Charity is **not**
    a. A great virtue
    b. Voluntary giving to the less fortunate, education, elimination of disease, or response to tragedy
    c. A personal choice to give to the causes that you are passionate about
    d. Best left for government to decide who gets money and who does not

6. English as the official language would
    a. Help unify our country
    b. Help immigrants to get good jobs in mainstream America
    c. Reduce dependency on the government
    d. All of the above

7. The primary function of the government is to
   a. Redistribute wealth
   b. Grant rights such as health care
   c. Keep people dependent on the government
   d. Protect and defend the constitution

8. Our current tax system
   a. Is too complicated to understand
   b. Costs billions of dollars a year to enforce
   c. Discourages people to make money and penalizes them for doing so
   d. All of the above

9. Your job as students is to
   a. Do your best in school
   b. Learn from a variety of sources
   c. Keep informed of current day events and get involved
   d. All of the above

10. "Fundamental change" should mean
    a. Government control of everything
    b. Huge government spending to control everything
    c. Massive taxes to pay for the control of everything
    d. Returning to the fundamentals of our founding fathers of small government and personal responsibility

1) b 2) d 3) d a (4 d (5 d (6 d (7 d (8 d (9 d 10) d
Answers:

INDEX

STEVEN ROTTER & BRADLEY ROTTER

L

Landrieu, Mary, 44
Lehman Brothers, 48

M

Medicare, 25
Mexico, 53, 70, 72, 74
Mitterrand, François, 32
Muslims, 55

N

Nelson, Ben, 44
No Child Left Behind, 67

O

Obama, Barack, 25, 27-33, 43, 47,
    58-59, 71
Occupational Safety and Health
    Administration (OSHA), 28

P

Pelosi, Nancy, 43

R

Reid, Harry, 43-44
Republicans, 43

S

socialism, 23-24, 30, 32
Stern, Andy, 30

T

trickle-down economics, 47

U

unions, 28-29
    problems with, 60-62
United States
    cultural divides in, 49-50, 52, 54, 56
    employment issues in, 62, 64, 66
    immigration issues in, 70, 72-73, 75-76

V

voting, 95

W

Washington, George, 21